An Adventure in Grief

Catherine de Courcy grew up in Dublin, graduated from UCD in 1979 and became a professional librarian. She worked in libraries in Ireland, Papua New Guinea and Australia. She travelled the Australian outback with her husband, John, and wrote several guidebooks. She has an international reputation as a historian of zoos. In 2003, some years after John's death, she returned to Ireland and is now a full-time writer.

An Adventure in Grief

Catherine de Courcy

The Collins Press

FIRST PUBLISHED IN 2009 BY
The Collins Press
West Link Park
Doughcloyne
Wilton
Cork

British Library Cataloguing in Publication Data
De Courcy, Catherine
Adventure in grief
1. De Courcy, Catherine 2. Johnson, John 3. Bereavement
4. Post-traumatic stress disorder 5. Veterans - Mental
health 6. Consolation
I. Title
155.9'37'092
ISBN-13: 9781905172870

Typesetting by The Collins Press
Typeset in Goudy 11 on 14 pt
Printed by CPI Cox and Wyman, UK

CONTENTS

1

THE END

I was making dinner when John went out to the barn to shoot himself. I put a pie in the oven, and followed him as far as the veranda. He was walking across the stony car-park of our property, trailing the high-powered rifle along the ground, his shoulders sagging.

'Dinner won't be long,' I called after him.

He vanished into the barn. I gave him a few minutes and then walked towards the barn to leave rubbish in the bin room behind it. It was an excuse to follow him.

'Comfort food, pie and chips,' I said in a conversational tone through the slatted door and walked on to dump the rubbish in a 44-gallon drum. I returned to the barn door. 'It will only be fifteen minutes, love.'

He said something and there was an almighty explosion. I heard an object fall.

I yelled at him through the green slats. There was no answer. I went to the side door of the barn; it was locked.

'You don't have to look', the thought ran through my head, 'you don't need to see this.'

I willed my legs to take me back into the house where I rang the first person who came to mind – John's mate from his Vietnam Veteran Welfare Association. Paul answered the phone.

'I think he's done it, I think he's shot himself. He's locked himself in the barn, I don't know for sure but I heard something fall.'

'Now is the time to ring the police.' Paul spoke calmly and with authority. This was his territory; he was a man in charge just like John would have been. He had dealt with numerous crisis situations involving veterans suffering from post-traumatic stress and there was no drama in his voice.

*

The police took forever to get to the house. Then a car came slowly across the mountain in the distance. I ran out to the road to hurry its approach. It pulled up under a tree out of sight of the barn.

'Come away from the house,' a uniformed policeman called. 'Get into the car. Where is the armed man at present?'
Armed man? John? I supposed in the circumstances he was. He could have been sitting in the barn deep in himself and looking down his rifle like he had done so often recently. I could not guarantee that he was actually dead and police are often shot in 'domestics' so they weren't taking any chances. Also John was a 'class one' shot and the police knew it, I had told them so on the phone the day before.

The policeman drove me back to a roadblock a kilometre down the road. There were several cars and about ten armed police in flak jackets at the block. I drew them a map of the house and gave as thorough a description of events as possible. Most of the police headed off into the forest towards the house.

It was evening but still bright. I sat in the car answering questions whenever they were directed towards me.

A couple of police returned from the forest.

'Your mud map doesn't match the house,' one of the police said, looking at me suspiciously.

I pride myself on my ability to draw a mud map and insisted it was accurate.

'Who's the woman in the kitchen?' another asked.

What?

'Is there another house between here and your house?'

'No . . . Yes, a small one in the trees,' I had to think about the presence of our nearest neighbour.

'Oh no,' one of them muttered, 'We've been surrounding the wrong house.' They just checked themselves from responding openly to the funny side of this. 'Hope the woman in there didn't notice.'

I sat at the roadblock. The police seemed to be waiting for the cover of darkness before approaching the barn. I could have stopped all of this by walking into the barn and checking for sure whether John had gone or not.

'He won't shoot me,' I said.

'We can't let you do that. We have a duty of care now that we're involved,' explained an older officer who had not left my side.

Two senior officers arrived, one of whom was a negotiator. He had an air of calm consideration about him as he stood by me. He drove me back towards the house and parked in the shadow of a tree. I could see the other senior officer approaching the barn from the side.

3

A few minutes later, the negotiator's two-way radio buzzed.

'. . . the deceased . . .'

The negotiator took my elbow gently. 'Let's go into the house now.'

*

That was in Australia in December 2000. Shortly afterwards I made a decision not to make any major decisions for two years but to take time to work through my grief. I had dodged grief once before, when my brother had died in 1984; now I was prepared to face everything that my response to John's death was going to throw at me. I suppose I could have moved country again and immersed myself in another distracting life but the part of me that was beyond emotional or mental cognisance was curious about how I would evolve if I faced the full onslaught of grief. Besides I had little else to do: I was alone in Australia with no responsibilities other than to turn up for work on schedule and pay bills. I was forty-three, the exciting life I had known with John was over, and I could live for another forty years or so. I was under no illusions but that grief was going to wreck me for at least the next year or two. However I hoped that if I collapsed into it rather than fighting it, perhaps by the end of the second year I might feel 'normal' again and maybe even have the basis for another life.

At the very least, this belief – or fantasy – was enough to get me out of bed in the mornings.

2

AFTERMATH

In the meantime, back on 7 December 2000, the negotiator steered me into the house and sat me on a sofa. A dozen police roamed around the house and gardens. Two looked intently at a photomontage on the wall.

I wondered what they were looking for. Signs of trouble? Evidence of culpability on my part? Checking there had not been a murder?

Frozen in colour were John and myself on the red dunes of the Australian outback, swimming off coral islands in the South Pacific, lyrical photos of me smiling at the camera, lyrical photos of John looking out over a sunset with a beer in his hand. Perhaps a trained eye could see something in this happy collection that foretold a violent suicide.

'There are two men at the roadblock who say they know you', said a policeman as he walked in off the veranda that surrounded the house. 'Warren and Garry. Do you want me to let them through?'

'Yes, please do.' They were my only friends on the

mountain, indeed my only friends within 120 km of where I was sitting. Our home was in the Strzelecki Mountains, east of Melbourne. Our working and social lives were still in Melbourne, where we had lived for twelve years before this. My family was in Ireland; John's family was scattered in Australia and Britain. We had only moved to this isolated property two years earlier as John was suffering increasingly from post-traumatic stress – brought on by his experiences in the Vietnam War – and he was finding it impossible to cope in the city.

'Mary must have contacted Warren and Garry,' I thought. After ringing Paul and the police, I had rung my sister in Ireland. She had talked to me while I waited for the police to arrive.

'I'd better ring her back and tell her John has actually done it,' I said aloud. The negotiator seemed used to people having a conversation with themselves, half out loud, half in silence. He handed me the phone. My sister, Brigie, answered.

'He's done it, he's shot himself in the barn,' I told her. I had no idea how that sounded at Brigie's end of the phone; I didn't even query what she was doing in Mary's house at 10 a.m., Irish time. 'Warren and Garry are on the way.'

Brigie took over ringing people in Ireland.

Who else should I ring?

'I need to let his son and daughter know.' His son, Robert, lived with his wife in Adelaide; Samantha lived with her partner and two-year-old son in Melbourne.

'We can send someone around to their houses,' the negotiator suggested. 'It's standard procedure,' he added when I hesitated.

'No, I'll ring Robert.' Adelaide was too far to send a police officer. 'But if you would let Samantha know, that would be great.' In some deeply illogical place I imagined that one of the police officers attending would drive to her house and tell her what had happened.

Warren and Garry came into the house and sat on either side of me. I was beginning to get very cold but could not move. The police continued to walk through each room, picking up things, looking in cupboards, even scrutinising the books on the shelves.

'We'll take you back to our house,' Warren said. 'The coroner has to send someone up so it will be some time before they can do anything with John. They suggest you don't go into the barn but just leave. They'll lock up.'

'I'll come back in the morning and sort things out here,' Garry added. 'I've been down to the barn. One of the lads said you should just burn it down, but I can clean it up, no worries.'

The barn was full of our camping gear as well as farm equipment. There were also fifteen 3-day-old chickens in a heated coop in the barn. They must have been traumatised by the blast.

'The baby chooks are fine for the night,' Garry continued. 'They're warm, have plenty to drink and eat and they're safe from the rats.'

Rats? I hoped John was safe from the rats too. Was there someone with him? Maybe I should be with him, stay with him until the coroner arrives.

'Before you go, we need to take away any medication that your husband was on,' the negotiator said.

I filled a large bag with John's supply of medication, wavering over his sleeping pills.

'We need it all, I'm afraid,' the negotiator was watching me closely.

Damn. I hoped they wouldn't spot Nelson's Valium on the shelf in the kitchen. Nelson, our dog, had died a few months earlier without finishing the full course of Valium prescribed to him; I was going to need something to help me sleep when everyone left.

Outside there were several police cars in the driveway. The light was on in the barn and the large doors were pushed open. I could have seen John if I looked but Warren steered me towards his car and turned on the heating full blast. By now I was so cold my teeth were chattering.

*

'I'm not sure what we are supposed to do in these circumstances,' Warren said. We were sitting by an open window in his house in the middle of a wood. There was music in the background and a fire blazing in the solid-fuel burner. 'Maybe I'll just go on putting these CDs together.'

He was preparing his Christmas presents, packaging a CD of his own original piano music. I remembered the strange combination of normality and extreme difference that filled the void after my brother, Mike, had died.

'Go for it,' I answered.

What was the alternative? Sit and stare at each other? Try to make conversation? Ordinary Christmas industry was a perfect distraction and gave me plenty of space to say as much or as little as I felt like.

I made several critical phone calls, to Robert, my parents, my close friend, Noeleen, in Ireland, and Brian, John's brother in England.

'John's shot himself in the barn,' I heard myself saying. I was insensitive to the drama I might be creating in their lives by this announcement.

It was too late to ring Australian friends, they would have to wait until morning.

At midnight, Warren gave me a Valium.

*

I lay in bed watching the tree outside the window until dawn. It was 5 a.m. in Australia and 6 p.m. in Ireland. The time difference was a blessing: night was not the enemy, just an opportunity to ring Ireland and talk, which I did for a couple of hours. Then I sat watching the birds and waiting for 8.20 a.m. when I could ring Maria, a woman in Ireland who sees the world from a different perspective and who I had met briefly on a visit to Dublin six months earlier. Noeleen had set up the phone call: 'Ring Maria at 9.20 p.m. her time,' she had said. 'She'll be waiting for your call.'

Maria's voice was warm and direct. 'Noeleen told me your husband, John, died last night.' She said a few things about John, about the troubles he had been carrying and how he had struggled with his load. 'For the last eight months he has been preparing to leave; he's been saying goodbye to old friends.'

That fitted: the previous March, we had had a family weekend on the farm with John's son, daughter, brother, their partners and John's grandson; it was the first and only time this group had ever gathered together. Since then John had spent time with old friends in Britain and Australia.

'And for the last month, he's been looking for the right time to leave,' continued Maria.

That fitted too: the last month had been hell. I did not query Maria's source of information. I could barely speak.

'Is he at peace?' I managed to get out.

'Well, he was hardly the peaceful sort, now was he?' said Maria shortly.

Of course he wasn't. I could not help smiling. Who was I trying to kid? John had been a gregarious character, a cheery, friendly person who engaged enthusiastically in whatever was going on around him. He always got up at the crack of dawn, sang in the shower, prepared traditional breakfasts at weekends using as many pots as he could lay his hands on, bought far too much food in the local markets and yelled at the television when he was watching football. His personality did not need to be reinvented just because he was dead. John was the liveliest, most exciting person I had ever met; he was certainly not one for dirge and melodrama. So to suggest that he might be lying peacefully somewhere suddenly seemed quite daft.

Maria talked more about John's troubles.

'Death is as much a part of life as living,' she added; her gentle matter-of-factness was soothing. 'It may be hard for you to see it right now but in time you will see the rightness of this.'

And at that moment I felt a great peace about John's death. Of course I had known he was going to kill himself, there was no point pretending otherwise. Life for the previous eighteen months had been a massive struggle for him. For the last month he had been wandering around the property firing the rifle without warning. Now it seemed like everything that had happened during that time was the course of a terminal illness that had come to its inevitable, sad end. It had been a complete nightmare but now it was over.

Or at least that part of it was over.

*

Shortly afterwards my sister Anna rang. 'Mary and I are coming out, we'll arrive in Melbourne tomorrow night.'

Heaven only knows how they managed to get flights in December at such short notice; flying in and out of Australia around Christmas without booking flights long in advance is always difficult. When I rang John's colleagues, my colleagues and our close friends in Melbourne during that morning, I was able to say that I was being very well looked after.

*

'How do you want to manage the funeral?' Warren asked over breakfast.

The funeral? Where was John now? Garry had gone back to the house to clean up the barn. I was sitting looking at the birds in the trees around Warren's house and was calm.

Neither John nor I belonged in Australia. John was originally from the north of England. He had run away from home when he was fourteen to train as a chef in London. He had left England forever at sixteen, under the auspices of the Big Brother Movement, an organisation that sponsored the emigration of British youths to Australia. For a long time he had had no contact with his family in England but had recently become close again to his brother. However he had never developed any affection for England again.

I belonged in Ireland. I had fled a land of economic misery, wet weather and corruption in the 1980s along with tens of thousands of other emigrants. My family was still in Dublin. John and I had met in Papua New Guinea in 1986 and moved to Melbourne in 1987. Although we had bought the property 120 km outside Melbourne in December 1998, we kept an apartment in Melbourne for overnight stays during the week.

So where would be the best place for a funeral and what would I do with John's body? Six hours before he died, he had said he wanted his ashes scattered on the Long Paddock, a wild paddock at the end of our property. Yet when we first met in New Guinea in 1986, he had told me he wanted to be buried at sea.

Decisions. I took a deep breath: 'the funeral will be in Williamstown, he'll be cremated – he wouldn't have wanted it otherwise – and I'll put his ashes out to sea.' Williamstown was close to Melbourne's city centre. We had lived there for nearly eleven years and it had a well-established funeral parlour so it seemed the logical place to have the funeral.

Warren made an appointment with a funeral director for the following afternoon. He also made an appointment for me to see Brenda, a therapist I had seen several times over the previous six weeks.

*

Garry rang from my house.

'It's going well,' he said. 'The police left me a bucket and some gloves. But there is a problem,' he hesitated as he sought the right words. 'I'm sorry I have to ask you this but whoever took John away last night left everything that was dislodged by the bullet lying on the ground. What do you want me to do with these remains?'

What indeed? Pack them up and take them to the rest of him? But where was the rest of him?

Garry offered some solutions; he had a medical background and was not fazed by the horror of this at all but understandably he did not want to make the decision himself. We agreed that Garry would bury the remains deep in the ancient rainforest adjoining the property and I returned to Warren's veranda to sit and watch the birds.

*

When I went home that evening, the place was quiet. Only a big hole in the barn door indicated that anything odd had happened here.

'I'm sorry I had to do that,' explained Garry. 'Those boards were closest to John when he shot himself; I couldn't clean them so I burnt them.'

He had done an amazing job. The chickens were safe and well, the place was tidy and even the barn looked benign.

Later that night I sat outside the barn in the dark looking at the big hole and trying to find some way of helping me feel what had happened. There was nothing.

'You took the ghost with you,' I said to John.

There had been a woman's ghost resident in the hundred-year-old barn, or so we had been told when we first moved there. Several visitors had sensed or heard it. Now I got it into my head that the explosion and the bullet going through the roof had somehow set her free.

I wondered where the bullet was.

I tried to think or to feel anything, but everything was blank. I gave up and went to bed, perching on the edge of my own side. I used to love it when John got out of bed at daybreak and I could roll into the middle and luxuriate in a sleep-in. Now all the space was my own but I could only lie on the edge.

I dreamt a man was holding me, stroking me very gently and I woke up feeling very loved. Then horror as the realisation dawned that John was dead and I seemed to be dreaming about another man already.

I sat on my veranda watching the sunrise over the orchard. There was silence.

3

THE FUNERAL

Warren drove me into Melbourne to see my therapist, Brenda, the funeral director and finally Samantha. Six weeks before John died I began seeing Brenda for no particular reason except that living with John was tough at times. Our first sessions had gone into the oddest of places. I had expected to talk about John, his mood swings and his deep sadness but Brenda had always shifted the conversation back to me and my responses. That Saturday Brenda was very gentle.

'We need to do a few things,' she said. 'First you need to say goodbye to him in his human form.'

She talked me through a sort of meditation and visualisation where I conjured up an image of John – very easily – said goodbye to him and walked away from him backwards. I could see him standing sadly in front of the barn, his shoulders drooping, his face forlorn, his eyes hopeless, and me walking backwards, looking at him with tears streaming down my face. Then in the visualisation I saw him turn towards the barn.

I stood looking at the barn and then, unexpectedly, John appeared again, this time peering around the side of the barn, beaming, looking young, cheerful and glowing. He came out and stood looking at me, smiling broadly. That was the John I had always known. There was a golden-white light about him. Then he vanished. I wanted him back.

Brenda gently brought me into another visualisation and this time I felt John around me, dancing. It was easy to go along with the visualisation – perhaps my mind was so dull that I was not being distracted with analysis.

'Ask him what he wants you to do about the funeral,' Brenda said quietly. I was still in that quiet, meditative place with my eyes closed.

I asked him and instantly an answer flashed through my head, 'When you're dead, you're dead. I don't care. Do whatever you like, love, it's up to you.'

'Great,' I couldn't help smiling as if the answer was real. 'You were supposed to help me make some decisions about this.'

Something very cheeky flashed through my head as an answer to that, leaving me feeling happy, as John would have done most of the time when he was alive. At that moment I realised that the man who had been holding me in my dream that morning was John. A powerful feeling of uncluttered love filled me. For that brief moment all of the difficult times of the previous eighteen months fell away.

*

The funeral people made it easy. John had paid for his own funeral, putting aside a small amount of money every year since he joined the Australian Army as a seventeen-year-old in 1964. There was plenty of money in the fund.

The funeral parlour could arrange everything from an elegant in-house chapel with an adjoining reception space to the Anglican priest who would officiate at the funeral. John had been of Anglican extraction and I wanted to have a religious element at the funeral. It was also to be a military funeral with a flag, medals, a photo of John in uniform and the Last Post.

'Come in to the back room and choose a coffin,' the director invited me.

Warren came also. The coffins were laid out on display with style names and price tags. The director left us to it. We were like a couple choosing a sofa in a department store.

'I was talking to Paul while you were in with the funeral director,' said Warren. Paul had been providing information about a charity for donations instead of flowers, which was required for the newspaper advertisement. 'He strongly recommended that you don't spend much money on the coffin because it will be covered in the Australian flag and burnt. Get the cheapest,' he suggested.

Oh, the practical Vietnam vets, John would have enjoyed that. But I had an image of what a coffin should look like and went with that regardless of cost. The fund was there to be spent.

'Do you want a video of the funeral?' the director asked when I was back in the office, the coffin selection made.

An instant response of 'no!' stopped before it came out. I had heard that it was common among European emigrants in Australia to video a funeral for family in the homeland so they could participate in someone's final ceremony.

'Yes, two copies please.' I never wanted to see it but would send it to my family and John's brother.

'Now, one final question,' said the director, looking at me carefully. 'We can arrange for you to see John in his coffin. There will be cloth over his face but you will see his hands. Do you want us to organise that?'

'Yes,' I said without hesitation. I really wanted to see John but had not thought that they would give me the option. I had no idea what condition he was in but I knew the importance of seeing the body of someone close who had passed way. When my brother, Mike, had died in a football accident in 1984, seeing him lying there, his nose blocked and not a mark on his body, had been critical to my eventual acceptance that he was dead. But when Nick, my first cousin, died in 1987, I was flying back in at the end of my contract in the University of Papua New Guinea. I got to the funeral mass in time but always regretted never having seen him laid out beforehand. I needed to see John actually dead.

An arrangement was made for the following Wednesday, the day before the funeral.

*

The final stop in Melbourne was to see John's daughter. Samantha and her two-year-old son, Jasper, had been regular visitors to the farm over the previous two years. She was aware how ill John had been so was shocked but not surprised that he had killed himself. I went through the detail of the lead-up to his death, answering her questions without reservation.

'When Jasper got up this morning,' Samantha said after we had exhausted the subject for the moment, 'he said he had been playing with granddad on the farm during the night. They played with the chickens and the ducks, and went up to the fence to talk to the sheep. He was chattering so happily, there was nothing dead about Dad to him. It was beautiful.'

John and Jasper had developed a form of communication based on a combination of enthusiastic cock-a-doodledoos, baas, quacks and moos. I had no doubt that John and Jasper had being playing somewhere during the night.

*

My sisters Mary and Anna arrived that night and took over. Now I could sit on the veranda, watch the butterflies and cockatoos and drink tea without interruption. It was very peaceful; all I could hear were the voices of my sisters and Warren and Garry in the air as they answered the phone, cleared out the barn, weeded the flower beds and made the place look tidy. They organised the funeral service, selecting music and readings. Warren, a church organist, was going to play some rousing, well-known hymns.

I wanted to end the funeral with a reel. I had been to the funeral of an elderly woman in Ireland where two musicians had played a reel at her graveside. It was so lively, it seemed to give the woman's spirit an opportunity to dance into heaven. I wanted that for John. Although his death was dramatic and suicide has immensely tragic associations, he was not a tragic person so it was not fitting that a man who had a jolly word to say to everyone should be sent off to the great unknown with a dirge.

*

On Wednesday we arrived at the funeral parlour to see John. Mary and Anna came in with me. Robert and Samantha had already seen him and were waiting in a nearby cafe with their partners and Jasper. A female funeral director greeted us.

'John is ready for you now,' she said calmly. 'But we were wondering if you would like to see him properly.' She paused, then continued. 'There are six women in this firm and thirty-seven men. The men didn't think you would want to see John with his head uncovered but all the women believed that you would. There is a bandage around his head. He doesn't look shocking at all.'

She waited for my reaction.

'Yes, I would like to see him.' I had no idea what I would encounter but it sounded like a challenge from John. He had spent fifteen years challenging me on all sorts of levels, physical, emotional and mental. I was not going to avoid this one just because he was gone.

John lay in a coffin at the top of the chapel. By the time I reached him I could barely see through the tears. The woman came in and removed the silk cloth from over his head. I couldn't help smiling at him as if he could see me from behind the wrapped bandage. His thick head of hair was still there and part of his forehead was visible. They had put his chin back together although not quite in the shape it originally was. I chuckled over that. It was lovely to see him there even if everything was blurry.

Mary and Anna left. I talked to him, stroking his hair and being careful not to let my hand go too far back down his skull. 'Small entry, big exit.' I recalled him demonstrating the characteristic damage that this type of bullet does. How much I had changed in the fifteen years I had known him.

That evening Robert and I sat in the plush dining room of the city hotel my sisters and I were staying in for the night, thanks to John's funeral fund. Robert had not seen John for months. He knew things had not been quite right with his father but had no idea how bad they had been. Now, surrounded by Christmas parties, we talked intensively until we ran out of energy.

*

The funeral was jam-packed. John's coffin was half-covered in the flag. 'Is that normal,' I wondered, 'or did they leave some of the coffin exposed because I picked a nice one?'

His service medals and a casual photo of himself in uniform sat on a small table in front of the coffin. John had been in the army for twenty-three years and had served in Vietnam in 1968–69 and in New Guinea before independence. This amounted to five impressive-looking medals.

At one point his veteran mates took over the funeral. Paul told a story about an incident in May 1968 when the Mini Tet Offensive had started. John was travelling through Saigon on a Defence Force bus full of Australian soldiers when a Vietnamese youth jumped at the bus and clung to the protective grid long enough to attach a satchel to it before vanishing. In a split second, a quick-thinking soldier unhooked the satchel – which contained an explosive device – saving John and everyone else in the bus from death or serious injury.

When Paul finished speaking the Last Post was played. Seventeen Vietnam veterans approached the coffin in twos, each paying their respects and dropping a red poppy into a gold tray in front of John. Their deep sadness was palpable in the chapel. Here was yet another of their mates who had either taken his own life or died prematurely of a physical ailment.

At the end of the service, 'John Doherty's Reels' played by Altan burst out over the chapel's loudspeakers. Tea and sandwiches were served in the adjoining reception room and then the hearse left for the crematorium followed only by myself, Robert and Samantha in the black funeral car.

*

Warren drove me and my sisters back to the house in the mountains. As we moved into the countryside, he turned on local radio. Minutes later the radio was playing 'Michael, Row the Boat Ashore'. That had been our brother's song as a child; we would have sung it on the seven-hour journey between Dublin and Roundstone in Connemara, County Galway, every summer. Never before or since have I heard that song played on radio. Now, here we were, me and my sisters sitting in the back with a bunch of flowers from my friends in Melbourne Zoo across our knees, Warren and Garry in the front, and Mike's childhood song being played for us on the radio. We joined in the harmonies as we might have done thirty or thirty-five years before. As far as I was concerned Mike was letting us know he was there also.

4

PEACE AND MEMORY

After the funeral, my world came to a halt. I retreated to the end of the veranda and sat watching the butterflies flitting around the orchard and the yellow-tailed black cockatoos swooping through the nearby forest. I was barely aware of Mary and Anna managing the house and the gardens. Sometimes I heard the phone ringing in the distance but someone else always answered it so it did not disturb me. It was a very peaceful time. I let snapshots of my life with John drift through my mind; sometimes they drifted on, sometimes I halted a thought or a memory and pondered on it.

'Why did this happen?'

But the question was obligatory rather than useful. I shrugged. To ask 'why?' suggested that something could have been different, but the damage had been done long ago and it was testament to John's spirit that he had stayed alive so long. We had been together for fifteen years and had had fabulous times together; there had been a lot of laughter, fun, joy, excitement, challenge and love. I did not want to lose any of that because of what had happened over the past fortnight or even during the eighteen months before that. If I could accept John's death as normal, the memory of our time together would not need to change. If I sank under the nature of John's death, there was a danger I might lose all of the goodness that had been in our relationship.

I could almost hear John getting cross: 'Don't give into melodrama, it doesn't suit you.'

The thought drifted on. The veranda overlooking the orchard wrapped me up in its safety and peace once more. I sat.

*

I had been lucky – more than lucky – meeting John in Papua New Guinea. Expat life in Port Moresby, the capital of Papua New Guinea, was pretty merciless. Expats were supposed to be self-sufficient and in control of their lives. When I arrived there in June 1985, I was twenty-six, couldn't drive, didn't have a credit card and was prepared to accept the first offer on everything, including accommodation, from the employer.

'You were such an airhead, a real dingbat', one friend said later. 'We were all watching in horror, wondering how long you'd last.'

A curfew was announced in Port Moresby the day I arrived. Gangs of young local men, known in pidgin English as *raskols*, had been terrorising the residents of Moresby. In response the government introduced a curfew, the practical implications of which were that anyone found on the streets between 10 p.m. and 6 a.m. would be arrested and have to spend the night in a police cell. The police also set up roadblocks on the main roads to check driving licences as a way of showing their presence on the streets. None of this bothered me; I was in an alien environment so, as far as I knew, everything I encountered was normal for the place. My immediate challenge was to establish the basics of living.

Within a few months I was driving, had set up my flat at the university and found the singles' social scene. There were about 25,000 expats in Moresby, many of them around my age and English-speaking. Socialising took place at the regular disco at the Royal Papua Yacht Club and in private groups – large parties, dinner parties in homes or restaurants, yachting and boating parties, pool parties, mountain treks, white-water rafting, wine-tasting events, horse racing and even rugby league matches. The lifestyle was seductive and there were plenty of invitations to exotic and indulgent events. It was also surprisingly accessible for someone like me with limited means and used to socialising on mountains, in pubs or at bridge parties. The Port Moresby expat world was a high-turnover society with low stakes in terms of socialising. Newcomers joined groups and either stayed if they merged well, or moved on to another group. There was no tension in this process because there was so little at stake; most of the people I mixed with were on contracts of two to five years and would never see each other again when they left the country.

At the beginning, it took a bit of practice to engage with the staple topics of parties where wine, food, travel and security dominated social conversation. Personal problems were also frequently raised in the company of semi-strangers. This was an aspect of expat interaction that continued to fascinate me. Coming from a country where no one talked much about how they were feeling about anything, it was both astonishing and riveting to be faced with dinner party conversations about domestic arguments, inability to have children, complaints about a partner who drank too much or squabbles over extended families.

*

In March 1986, I met John on a local scuba-diving course when my friends Jason and Sally encouraged me to join in this popular expat activity. The rich coral reefs were close to the shore, there was great visibility, diverse reef structures, loads of fish and shells, and the water was warm enough not to require a wetsuit. It was also safe: the raskols could not get us out on a boat. On my first dive I could not get my ears to clear and was floating in mild frustration on the surface while my fellow students vanished underwater.

'Come on, Irish.' John bobbed up from underneath the water wearing his mask. 'You'll get sunburnt if you sit on top of the water all day. Grab hold of my hand, we're going down.'

He brought me down towards a sunken trawler sitting on the seabed about ninety feet under water. A grouper swam beside us, John stroked it and invited me to do the same. The big, ugly-looking fish looked soft but felt very solid. John fed it with food from the net hooked to his belt. The fish took the food, then rubbed itself along John as we swam on. When we arrived at the trawler, the other students were leaving. John sat in front of the cabin and pulled more food out of his net. A moray eel appeared and grabbed at his hand. John gestured to me to feed the eel.

'Good one, Irish,' he declared when we resurfaced, 'but wash your face before getting back on the boat, your nose is dribbling.'

'That's our Johnno,' said Tom, the dive master, looking over the back of the boat. 'Likes nothing better than to help out a damsel in distress.'

*

John Johnson, or Johnno as he was known on the boat, was popular in this diving circle. Besides being loud, cheerful and inclusive, he was a very keen diver and spent most weekends on the dive boat, helping out as an assistant instructor in exchange for free dives. During the week John was an officer with the Australian Army, posted to work with the Papua New Guinea Defence Force for two years. He had taken up diving after separating from his wife a year before and, at thirty-six, he was a skilled and confident flirt.

'Another hour before the next dive and it's a beautiful day for sunbathing. Would you rub this on my back?' he asked holding out a bottle of suntan cream. He spent the next hour sunbathing beside me with barely a word.

'Drinks in the Yacht Club,' John announced to everyone on the boat at the end of the second dive. There were about twenty students and ten volunteer crew. 'You coming, Cath?'

The Yacht Club was lit by candlelight that evening. There had been a power cut so the normally grey atmosphere in the concrete building overlooking the harbour was almost romantic. The conversation turned to the forthcoming St Patrick's Day party being organised by my Irish friends.

'Come back to my house, I can give you green clothes,' John offered loudly.

'Phooar, Johnno, you're some operator,' said one of several lads who had been monitoring John's move on me.

I ignored them. In Moresby, expat lives were lived in goldfish-bowl conditions but there was such a high turnover of people that it didn't matter. I followed John back to his house and, as he would later tell the story, never left.

*

'If I hadn't followed him home that night, where would I be now?' I wondered.

'You daft bugger, it's far too late for what-ifs. You're indulging again,' a response came instantly.

I looked around. It was easy to imagine that John was sitting at the end of the veranda talking to me.

'Don't get carried away,' I warned myself. We had been together for so long that it would have been easy to fill in his responses to my thoughts and have a lengthy conversation.

Yet if he were really here, it would be perfection. He would not be carrying the weight of trauma any more and I would not have to worry about his demons setting him off. In this little slice of heaven, our relationship could be pure and total. I felt warm and safe and light-headed. I had never experienced this total feeling of peacefulness in my life before. I could have remained here forever.

5

REALITY CHECK

Footsteps on the veranda. 'Cath, you need to make some decisions.' It was Mary. 'You have to come back into the world. I'm only here for a few more days and I'd like to think you'd have some control of your life before I leave.'

'Do I have to? Not yet, surely?' I tried to focus. 'I can't think at the moment. I'm OK here; it's safe. Please, I'll be fine.'

'No, you won't. You have to connect, even a bit.'

Mary was gently persistent. As a psychotherapist, she knew what she was talking about. Warren and Garry had gone back to their own lives. Anna was staying on for several more weeks. I had not really registered how much they or Mary and Anna had been doing for me. I was barely present; physically I was there but I think most of the rest of me had floated out after John into the unknown.

'Why don't we do a plan of what you have to do?' suggested Anna. 'We could identify key objectives and put optimal timelines against them.'

Clever move, she knew exactly how to make me focus. For a number of years I had worked in the State Library in Melbourne as a reference librarian and trainer. One of my more recent jobs was to train the staff, over 300 people, in work management and planning techniques. Anna was talking a language I understood and could use on automatic pilot.

The list of objectives was lengthy and the completion dates extraordinarily ambitious; it included selling the farm and the second car, getting the city apartment onto the market, organising a solicitor to do probate, cancelling credit cards, putting everything into my name, getting a handle on my financial situation, renting a two-bedroom apartment in Melbourne and many minor things. And we planned to do all of that before Anna left the country in the middle of January.

*

Christmas approached – a terror for the recently bereaved. The first Christmas after Mike died had been distressing; the traditions that had once made Christmas so warm and pleasant had turned the season into a difficult time. John would be dead just over three weeks on Christmas Day. Fortunately I had mastered the art of Christmas long ago by treating it simply as a special day involving good food, interesting wine and warm company. John and I had had fabulous Christmases together but we had not established any traditions. John had never had joyful Christmases growing up in the north of England. His parents, both heavy drinkers, had been careless of providing gifts or meals to their three children. From the age of seven, when his mother turned to alcohol, John had managed the cooking and other domestic aspects of the household. John and his younger brother would fish or kill pigeons to provide a meal. Sometimes – particularly around Christmas – they would risk severe violence by removing coins out of their father's pocket to buy a chicken.

John and I had often gone to the Australian desert for Christmas and New Year. At other Christmases we had joined friends; sometimes his children had joined us and once we were with my family in Ireland but whatever the company or location, it had always been a day of no fuss and no drama. So that was the way it would be this year. Anyway, I was too blitzed to notice much about Christmas Day. And Anna, who had lived abroad for a number of years also, did not seem to mind the absence of a ceremonial day.

*

New Year's Eve threatened to be much more difficult but Warren and Garry organised a party in their forest home. Warren played a medley of popular songs on his grand piano, then broke into 'You'll Never Walk Alone' from the musical *Carousel*. I was on their veranda looking at the stars and, just like the scene from the musical when the ghost of Billy Bigelow talks to his wife, I imagined John urging me to sing the words. '*When you walk through a storm, hold your head up high* . . .' John loved musicals; he had had a terrific music-hall voice and would have made an excellent 'Ruler of the Queen's Navy'. As a motivational song with mountains of emotion, 'You'll Never Walk Alone' was undoubtedly a good one – '*At the end of the storm is a golden sky* . . . ' Warren played on, repeating the song several times. I wrapped the spirit of John around me and watched the stars.

*

The administrative objectives worked out with Anna were completed on schedule, which would have been remarkable in normal circumstances. Farms in that part of Australia can take up to two years to sell. Mine sold within ten days with a March settlement date. I found a perfect two-bedroom apartment in a desirable corner of town between the busy food-strips of Fitzroy Street and Chapel Street; unusually for that part of town, it had a substantial, secure car park suitable for the large outback vehicle that had been John's pride and joy, and which I wanted to keep. Anna got a good price for the second car. The city apartment was put in the hands of a trustworthy estate agent. Jason rang from London to ensure I had enough money to handle immediate expenses. And John's work colleagues went far beyond the call of duty to assist me in managing my financial affairs.

Paul made sure that John's death was considered war-related so I could be declared a War Widow as quickly as possible. This gave me loads of concessions, including travel and total medical cover as well as a small pension. It felt weird to be called a widow at 43 years of age and even weirder to be called a war widow. But there was no point in making a fuss, they were just words.

Mary and Anna had restored the barn door so there was no visible evidence of John's death. Together with Warren and Garry, they had systematically moved through the house, the barn and farm sheds, preparing the property for sale. Everything that had been damaged when John shot himself had been burnt. Things of John's that I would not use and did not want to keep were given to good homes. The sheep had been sold. The whole place was clean and uncluttered.

The bank was the only organisation to give me trouble. At first their communications were merely without grace and contained no acknowledgement of my loss. Government departments and other organisations managed to slip in a line at the beginning of their letters expressing condolences before getting into the technical stuff. But not the bank. Then the carelessness started. A steady stream of letters or statements addressed to 'The Estate of John Johnson' and starting 'Dear Mr Johnson, thank you for your recent enquiry ...' or offering an opportunity to win a holiday in Hawaii was initially tolerable, then bizarre and, as the months wore on, enough to make me angry.

6

TRAVELLING WITH JOHN

Anna left Australia and I went back to work. The physical impact of grief was unexpectedly powerful; each day was a massive struggle and I found it impossible stay alert for more than four or five hours at a time. The library was fairly quiet; it was January, the traditional time for lengthy summer holidays, and there were few people around so I took advantage of the library's flexitime system and went home early whenever I could. It was seven weeks since John had died yet waves of dizziness continued to pass through me frequently and without warning. My colleagues were very supportive and quickly agreed that I would work only three-day weeks for a number of months. I retreated to the farm as soon as I could and sat peacefully again watching the butterflies among the lemon and apple trees. The landscape was pristine and the air very silent.

I spent every four-day weekend at the farm until the beginning of March when the settlement on the sale came through. John's vegetable garden was rich with organic cabbages, peppers, tomatoes and other vegetables. The twenty-five trees in the orchard were overloaded with fruit, the gardens were in bloom and the paddocks were growing. It was exactly as John had planned it. The idea of moving to the farm had been to create a long-term home on the mountain. John had planned to go on working until his mid-fifties when he could draw on his various pensions and superannuation funds. In the meantime he would develop the farm, orchard and gardens so that when he retired he could spend his time growing and making his own foods.

Two years after he started his hard work had paid off – but of course he was not here to experience it. That made me feel very sad for him. 'Maybe if he'd held on . . .'

But there was no question of it and that train of thought was not going anywhere useful. There were plenty of other thoughts that allowed me to tap into John's presence again.

*

John and I had had an exciting and busy time in Papua New Guinea together. On the one hand it seemed a long time ago, on the other it felt as if it were only yesterday. John knew about food, wine, socialising, travelling, rugged bush adventure and all of the other activities that fuelled expat life in Moresby. He also spoke fluent pidgin English, one of Papua New Guinea's national languages, and could communicate easily with local people. He brought me into markets to get strange vegetables and fresh fish. He chatted endlessly and with great humour with the stall-holders. There was plenty of laughter.

John's house was standard for Australian officials in Port Moresby. His bedroom was lined with steel, there were metal bars on the slatted windows, a peephole in the heavy metal bedroom door, emergency buttons, a siren on the roof, radio control to the Australian High Commission, electronic gates and an eight-foot fence with razor wire around the property. Yet the house was also an elegant place with polished floorboards, two bedrooms, a large, well-equipped kitchen and a very large living and dining area that was ideal for parties.

John's local 'houseboy', Moxy, lived in a house in the substantial back garden. Moxy's extended family often stayed there so, at any one time, there could have been fifteen people on the property. Four properties adjoined ours. They all had 'boy-houses' in the back garden with large families living there. John knew them all, exchanged friendly conversations in pidgin and bought local food from them. He once put on a *mumu* or local feast for Moxy, his family and all of the neighbours.

*

John was the same on our travels. Our first holiday together was a six-week plane hop through Indonesia, which started in the volatile region of Irian Jaya. When we disembarked, four Indonesian soldiers were standing close to the bottom of the steps with their rifles trained on the queue of exiting passengers.

'Just keep walking, don't pay any attention,' said John to me quietly. He knew soldiers, rifles and violent tension so I trusted him to read the situation.

That evening we became stranded 40 km from our hotel when everything suddenly closed down at 10 p.m. We had been so carried away by the vibrant markets of brightly coloured vegetables and fake watches in the nearby city of Djaypura that we had lost track of time and missed the last bus out to our hotel in Santori near the airport. A taxi took us part of the way there, leaving us in a suburban street 20 km from our destination. There was no sign of life on the road except for a soldier with a machine gun who was waiting forlornly nearby in the hope of hitching a lift. A young man appeared from a house and offered us a lift in a friend's taxi for a reasonable price, which we gratefully accepted, but as we approached the white mini-van, two more young men appeared and moved towards the van also.

'Taking a crowd, are we?' said John. 'That's ok, but we'll take that soldier as well.'

'Mate,' John stood at the van door blocking the extra passengers' way and called to the soldier. 'Santori?'

The soldier joined us willingly and settled on the back seat with John and me. The English-speaker in the front seat grinned and shrugged.

'I am a major in the Australian Army,' John told the soldier in an effective combination of English, Indonesian, gestures and tone.

The soldier understood; he straightened up.

'Your rifle, the safety switch is off, that's dangerous, no good.'

The soldier understood again. He pointed out to the dense wood we could just see through the dark, then drew his finger across his throat. At the end of the trip, we jumped out and paid the English-speaker who grinned broadly at John. It did not take much to work out that the soldier with his loaded and cocked rifle had, at the very least, saved us from being robbed by our unwanted taxi companions. John's confidence in dangerous situations made me feel both safe and exhilarated.

*

The remainder of that holiday in Indonesia was full of exotic sensations. We ate frequently at food stalls by the side of the road.

'Always go for the stir-fry,' advised John. 'It's freshly cooked in boiling oil and won't give you Bali Belly. Eat loads of hot chilli to kill off anything dangerous and whatever you do, don't wash your teeth in the tap water.' Once I did and was very ill for a couple of days.

We went on boat trips, surfed and went scuba diving. In Manado, we were invited to a local wedding where, to my intense embarrassment and John's delight, we became instant guests of honour. John danced with a stream of women of all ages, I sat and smiled, exchanging as much chat as I could manage with the group of local girls who sat around me waiting for their turn on the dance floor with John. By this stage he knew enough Indonesian words to chat confidently.

We were in the grimy oil town of Banjarmasin on 17 August, Indonesia's Independence Day. We left the hotel at about 10.30 a.m. and found a ceremony under way in the bank next door. Smartly dressed dignitaries, men and women, were sitting in the portico of the bank. Six healthy-looking cows were tethered by the gate. John went straight up to them and stroked each in turn. He chatted with the young lads hanging around.

'Those poor, dumb animals,' John translated what they were saying for me. 'They're going to have their legs pulled out from under them and will probably break their ribs when they crash to the ground. Then their throats will be slit. The drain in this corner is to catch the blood. The meat will be distributed among the local people.'

John whispered to the cows and stroked them for half an hour until the males in the ceremonial party left the portico and moved towards the animals. The young men stood up, preparing to pull at the ropes.

'I can't watch, let's go,' said John with tears in his eyes and an expression on his face that was a cross between anger and sadness.

We walked on and spotted hundreds of people going down a road. Most were wearing blue batik shirts. We followed them. An army officer stepped out to block our way. He was an intimidating sight in mirror glasses, a big peaked hat, masses of gold braid around his lapels, and medals. His English was limited.

'No more, forbidden,' he commanded, gesturing at us to stop.

John said something to him and walked around him. I followed hesitantly, expecting some terrible response from the officer.

'No photos,' the army officer called after us as we made our way to a low rise.

'Johnson, that was cheeky, are you sure it's OK?' I asked, as we continued walking.

'Don't worry; despite all that gold braid and stuff, he is only a lieutenant. He was just throwing his weight around. If tourists weren't allowed to watch the parade, there wouldn't be any others here at all. Relax.'

What a man! He outranked the lieutenant and was not going to take any orders from him even if they were not in the same army. A few days later, in Surabaya, we encountered another army officer. We were taking photos of a large mansion across expansive grounds when a black Mercedes with darkened windows turned into the gate and stopped. The back window slid down and John was summoned by a distinguished-looking man in civilian clothes. They had a friendly conversation before the Merc drove into the property.

'OK, love, let's move on, no more photos.'

'And how come you are obeying this time?'

'Brigadier.' This time John was outranked. 'And it's the governor's residence, so fair enough.'

*

Our final destination before returning to Port Moresby was in Ujung Pandang on the island of Sulawesi. There we befriended two Americans, Sam and Lizzie, who had been sailing around the world for a while. Lizzie's husband had died a few years earlier of cancer at the age of thirty. Sam was an old friend of the couple. They invited us back to their yacht at the edge of the harbour for a nightcap.

'I can't believe this is our last night. I don't want to go back,' said John, becoming upset; he looked sad and vulnerable. 'That music is beautiful, would you turn it up?'

It was 'Chung Kuo' from *China* by Vangelis. We sat watching the sun set into the sea with the delicate sounds of *China* filling the air. An anchored dhow was the only interruption between us and the golden horizon.

'You're very sad,' Lizzie said to John, who was now sobbing quietly.

'I don't want to go back, I don't want this to end. I've lost my family, I'm tired of the army, I'm tired of the rat race, I just want to sail out into the sunset and keep sailing.'

The look in his eyes suggested he very far away. He let the tears roll down his cheeks. Sam and Lizzie sat steadily, John's sadness did not distress them. They refilled our glasses and replayed *China* several times over while the glow settled into darkness.

I played 'Chung Kuo' at John's funeral.

7

LEAVING THE FARM

One Sunday in February I was on the veranda as usual and Garry was doing the final clean-out of the barn. This included moving a box freezer.

'Cath, I've found something,' Garry called.

He walked over holding the object in the palm of his hand.

'I think the rats must have got it, used it for a nest probably. I didn't know whether to give it to you or not but decided I should.'

Slowly it dawned on me. Garry was holding a sizable piece of John's skull and several smaller pieces. I felt a panic attack coming on but stopped it – it would not be fair on Garry if I collapsed in front of him. I wrapped the pieces in a handkerchief and put them into one of John's hats. John had a great hat habit and bought several hats in Ireland, including a tweed, peaked cap. It seemed the appropriate place to store a section of his skull.

I waited until Garry left, then collapsed. What does one do with a large piece of skull? I could imagine John telling me not to be a nervous Nelly and to stop making an unnecessary drama out of this.

'It's just bone,' he would have said. 'Deal with it and move on.'

A panic attack began to rise again. My breathing was getting short, my chest tight and my brain was seizing up.

'Love, now come on.' This time I seemed to hear him. There was a sense of urgency in the words, the same urgency he used whenever we had found ourselves in an extreme situation in the desert. 'What are you at? It is just bone. It can't bite. The only drama about it is the drama you create yourself. Stop acting and work it out.'

I tried to control the panic.

'I'm bloody entitled to cry,' I shouted. 'If I want to react to a piece of your skull appearing from nowhere, I will, so shut up and go away.'

The shouting interrupted the rapid breathing and the panic attack subsided. I had to drive 120 km back to Melbourne later that day so could not indulge in a Valium. Fortunately *Calamity Jane* was on the television and I let Doris Day and Howard Keel calm me to a safe level.

Then it struck me: John had said he wanted his ashes scattered on a remote part of the property. I had collected the box containing his ashes a week earlier; the man who retrieved them from the funeral parlour's store had appeared at the reception desk whistling merrily with a parcel on his shoulder. 'Here you go,' he said plonking the parcel on the desk. 'Sign here.' He reminded me of a Cockney extra from *Oliver* but I resisted smiling at the incongruity of the scene until I was outside. John's ashes were now sitting in a dull orange plastic container on a bookshelf where I could see them. I was waiting for Robert and Samantha to be available to scatter them at sea.

I had no intention of scattering his ashes on the property. Firstly, the ashes did not resemble the fine grey ash depicted in the movies: their texture resembled kitty litter and might have been visible in the paddock; and secondly, I could never visit the paddock after I left. Putting his ashes out to sea meant that I could visit him at any ocean in the world.

So now angels – I preferred that image to rats – had presented me with a small part of John that I could place in a remote part of the property and fulfil his last request.

'You rotten sod, you set this up!' I imagined him enjoying this. Through all of the chaos of his life and death, I was beginning to believe that John had managed a degree of control over the whole situation to make it easy for me. He had chosen a way to kill himself that had given me the least trauma: I had been able to hear him but not see him so I did not have to face the horror of the immediate aftermath yet I had no outstanding questions. He had made sure I had been strong enough to see him in his coffin with just a bandage wrapped around his head. He had made sure I was now safe with close friends around me. And now he had given me a piece of him to scatter on the property and honour his wishes.

'That's my man.' I felt pleased and privileged at having been married to a man who could still manipulate things in my favour after his death. There seemed to be no boundaries between life and death any more. Our journeys were still running parallel to each other and we were still travelling together; he was no longer making footsteps but that was only because he was in a dimension I did not understand yet. I was in no mood to doubt his ability to influence earthly matters from where he was now. Nor was I in a mood to question my mental health. 'So maybe I am going off the rails', the thought occurred to me periodically but each time I dismissed it quickly. I was aware that some of my behaviour might have raised concerns in others if they had seen it but there was no one to judge me on top of the mountain and, if anyone was worried about me, I was unaware of it.

For the next few weekends I lit enormous fires in the solid wood burner in the house and gradually, very slowly, reduced the bone of John's skull to pieces that would not spark off a murder hunt if they were ever found. I went as far as I could into the ancient rainforest on the edge of the property to scatter the little bits of bone.

*

In the end I left the farm, ready to go. For the first time since we had been on the farm a possum had got into the roof several times and played with the electric cords, creating a racket and making me nervous. Lethal snakes suddenly began to appear; this was snake country and several local snakes were particularly dangerous. They had never bothered me before but now several appeared in ways that made me feel vulnerable. Then smoke from a bush fire wafted over the house. This was also bush-fire country but the house had been standing for over a hundred years so I had never worried about the threat when John had been alive. Now I was shaking so much that I could not find the phone number of the local police station. I rang Warren who ascertained that the fire was under control.

'Enough,' I yelled at John and the heavens, 'I've got the message, I'm leaving.'

*

The farm changed hands on 7 March, the three-month anniversary of John's death and the day chosen by the Australian White Wreath Association to draw attention to suicide in the community by placing hundreds of white wreaths on the lawns in front of the State Library. Tables displaying information and photos about suicide greeted me when I arrived at work. For the first time it occurred to me that perhaps the circumstances of John's death were no longer unique but part of a wider issue. Traditional concepts like tragedy, guilt and stigma came to mind.

It had not occurred to me that there should be any guilt for anyone around John's death and to add a sense of stigma would be to undermine his decision. In John's case suicide was just his way to die. I did not know enough about the subject to pronounce on it for anyone else but I could not think of John's death as a tragic suicide. Perhaps I was deluding myself. Would I one day be faced with unidentified horrors that a husband committing suicide traditionally presented? Was that a reality I was currently avoiding? But right now, three months after he died, I could not imagine what the horrors were and was happy to stay deluded.

'That's OK for me,' the thought struck me. 'But I've thrown my own family in at the deep end of a great personal tragedy.' It suddenly became very important that they should know of the lead-up to and the circumstances of John's death. I made plans to visit Ireland in May when, hopefully, the two months' grace would give me enough energy to make the trip. Right now it was tough enough getting a tram to work each morning.

Walking past the wreaths on the way into the Library I glanced at the faces staring out of the photos on the White Wreath Association posters; they looked terrifyingly young to have made such a monumental decision as to kill themselves. Had they exhausted every possible way of sorting themselves out before making their final decision, I wondered? Or had they killed themselves early on in their troubles? It became too much to carry into work and I left at 3 p.m. that afternoon, desperate for a Valium and a dose of Gene Kelly dancing his way through *Brigadoon*.

8

GRIEF EMERGING

John vanished when I left the farm. I could no longer sense him or hear him. I tried visualising or hearing him but failed. Looking at photos or home movies made no difference – I could have been looking at a stranger. A few years before he died we had been on a television chat show when our travel book *Desert Tracks* was published. I watched that recording but could not recognise his face or his voice. It became so stressful that I put the photos and videos away.

But once I did hear him loud and clear. It was after an earlier incident on a tram when a ticket inspector had questioned my War Widow's travel concession card on the way to work one morning. The tram had been full and the inspectors had boarded in their usual pack of three or four. They were involved in a running battle with fare evaders and their patience was limited. I produced my ticket.

'Have you got your concession card?'

I produced my War Widow's travel concession card.

'What's this? This isn't on the list.'

Bored passengers looked up lazily, anticipating a distracting confrontation between an errant passenger and aggressive ticket inspectors.

'What's a war widow? This isn't a concession card.' She was talking out loud. She called the team leader. They pored over the card, discussing it. With some polite explanation on my part, then a threat to ring their customer service office, they eventually agreed to accept it.

I was so upset that I would have gone home if I had not had a meeting that day. I rang the ticketing company's customer service people to tell them to upgrade their training. The customer service officer was sufficiently apologetic to diffuse the situation yet such was my state of mind that the incident rattled me for weeks. Every time I got on the tram I expected a row. Arguments with phantom ticket inspectors ran around and around in my head. I knew it was bonkers but I couldn't stop them.

Then one day going into work on an almost empty tram, a loud message interrupted yet another round of imaginary arguments. 'They're only doing their jobs,' the message said. It was so clear it could almost have been a voice. It had to be John, it was exactly what he would have said. He had always been very assertive and fair in his transactions. Of course the ticket inspectors were only doing their jobs. John – or my memory of him – was telling me to let it go. Remarkably, given my state of mind, that particular argument vanished from my repertoire.

*

Work continued to be a trial. Although I had taken seven weeks' leave after John died and was only working three days a week for the present, it was hard to concentrate for any length of time. It also seemed very difficult to communicate clearly about even the simplest of things. These reactions were quite distressing. If I could have accepted that this state of mind was simply part of a grief process, I might have relaxed into it. However it did not feel part of a temporary condition, it just felt incompetent and dozy.

'My brain is mush,' I wrote to one of my sisters. 'I have to listen very carefully to what someone is after. I can't work on automatic. And I think I am making ghastly errors of judgement when I am talking to people. My big fear is talking too much about John and his death. I have a terrible fear that I will bore or frighten or something in between by talking too much about him to colleagues. I have to develop techniques to shut up.'

Warren worked down the road and met me regularly for lunch, debriefing me when I was completely wound up.

'Cath,' Warren said, 'You realise that most people will expect you to be over it by now. John died nearly four months ago. They won't have any idea that you are in such a state. So don't worry about it.'

Colleagues who were friends also took me away for coffee periodically to calm me down. Every diversion was a blessing. The project I was working on was politically charged so I focussed all my energy on that and let other aspects of my work take their course.

*

At home in the apartment in Windsor, life was easier because I could go to bed and doze or watch videos. My body was constantly sore and jittery, my head pounded most of the time and I developed odd headaches that could not be managed by aspirin or paracetamol. I was barely sleeping at night but that did not bother me. I bought two soft feather pillows, a warm duvet and an electric blanket with dual control; it was still summer but I was constantly cold. I left one side of the blanket on 'low' all night so that the empty half of the bed was never cold; I still could not sleep in the middle.

When I was not sleeping, I lay on my soft pillows telling myself this was a common symptom of grief and not to fight it. When I did sleep, my dreams were very busy, sometimes leaving me exhausted in the morning. Transport-related scenes featured frequently in my dreams. The transport involved cars, trams, trains, taxis, bicycles and once, to my bemusement, a horse and carriage. The scenes seldom involved getting to the destination safely or easily; more often than not I did not arrive at my destination at all. The dreams often involved scenes where the transport was out of control or I was lost, muddled or on the wrong route. Sometimes I got very angry in the dreams; this was distressing and I usually woke up feeling particularly unsettled. I got so used to the transport dreams that each morning when I registered the dream, I observed the mode of transport and noted how unsuccessful the journey had been.

A doctor had given me sleeping pills and Valium when Nelson's leftover supply ran out. I used half a sleeping pill if I wanted to treat myself to a blank four or five hours' sleep. They would make me groggy the next day so I had to plan this particular treat carefully and never before a work day.

The Valium served a different purpose. On my days off I often had massive crying fits where I would be on the ground wailing and wanting to crawl under the bed – which had about one inch of clearance. My body would be wracked in pain from the sobbing but remarkably there was never any story in my head other than wonderment about how long I could take the physicality of the fit and curiosity as to why it always seemed necessary to wail on the floor. I even tried to conjure up feelings of 'it's not fair. Why should this happen? Why did he do it?' and so on but my head was pretty clear on the matter: any ideas like that were made up. I had no angry stories for these occasions, just observation about how long my body could put up with the convulsing punishment.

As soon as the wailing stopped naturally or I judged that I had had enough, I would take a low-level Valium to calm down. On one occasion I could not stop at all and ended up taking three Valium to try and curb the fit. Mostly, however, the tears and emotion would be spent and I could slide into bed, get warm and, if the Valium kicked in, doze off.

I never had these fits if someone else was present: it might have worried them. In fact I avoided getting upset in company. Most of the time it was easy enough to switch that side of me off. There was no point in dragging anyone into this heavy-duty emotion, there was nothing they could do to lift my pain. This was entirely my business and I had to hope that something was working its way out of my system during these fits.

*

The mail was a bit of a nightmare because it generally meant more administrative work, more things to be read and signed, more phone calls to make, more death certificates to be sent, more letters to be written. It was endless.

An inordinate amount of things seemed to go wrong with otherwise routine administration. The police had sent me two letters looking for John's rifle, which they had taken away the night he died. The bank's incompetence had achieved a life of its own. Now they could not work out how to reimburse me for several months' accident insurance that they had charged the Estate of the Late John Johnson.

The lawyer doing the conveyancing on the sale of my city apartment was having trouble with the paperwork. Our city apartment was a one-bedroom apartment in the central business district so was ideal for its original purpose as an overnight stop but not right as a permanent home. Jack, the city-based agent, was selling it for me. I asked the lawyers who were handling probate to direct me to one of their conveyancing staff. It gradually dawned on me that the assigned lawyer was either on work experience, in her first job or supremely incompetent. Her paperwork was often incomplete and Jack would not accept it.

'Oh it doesn't matter,' said the lawyer. 'The agent will know what I mean.'

Jack, understandably, was furious. 'This is outrageous. I can't close on this apartment if the paperwork isn't correct. Tell her she has to do it properly.'

The phone calls went on for a fortnight and took on monumental proportions in my head. Surely this was a simple task. Why could an expensive lawyer in a reputable firm not get it right? Was my agent overreacting?

The stress built.

'Either some of the people I am dealing with are genuinely incompetent,' I tried to reason this through, 'or I am too flaky to focus properly and am making mistakes in my communications. Or I am the one making the mountain out of the molehill. Or maybe it is because there is so much administration, it is likely that some things can go wrong. Law of averages and all of that.'

But a bank charging a dead person accident insurance, police looking for a rifle they had presumably removed for forensic examination after a suicide, and a lawyer who didn't believe complete paperwork was necessary: what was going on? Was the universe trying to tell me something? Was this like the snakes, the possum and the fire at the farm? Was I in such a state that the universe had found cracks in my system and was taking advantage of them? Or was I now completely paranoid and looking for meaning when there wasn't any?

I retreated to *Kiss Me Kate*. Howard Keel and Kathryn Grayson in full voice were guaranteed to drown out the noise of incompetence and/or addled bereavement.

Correct paperwork was eventually squeezed out of the lawyer. The police stopped annoying me. And as for the bank, that went on for over a year; I eventually learnt to use it as an anger management exercise.

*

I established some pleasant routines for my life in Melbourne's inner suburb of Windsor. It was close to Albert Park and St Kilda. Although it is only a few kilometres from the city centre, St Kilda has a distinctive atmosphere with attractive beaches, palm trees, a pier, gardens and cafes. It also has a seedy element to it with street prostitution and drugs. There are numerous hostels in the area, some for backpackers, others for people down on their luck.

On days off and weekends, walking across Albert Park to the beach, watching the sun set over the water, paddling ankle deep as it became dark and getting a takeaway from one of the cheap, good-quality restaurants along Fitzroy Street became a routine way of passing the evening. I would turn on the TV for company and sound as soon as I walked in the door. As well as watching 1950s musicals, several television programmes like *Neighbours*, *Law and Order* and *Dalziel and Pascoe* became my friends.

Warren had taken up the spare room in the apartment for two or three nights a week – he worked three or four days a week in Melbourne and spent the rest of his time in the mountains. He was a wonderful friend to have around and, I am sure, saved me from complete insanity by his caring but unobtrusive presence.

'If I see you "going over the top", or indulging in a "poor me" widow scenario,' he said once when I asked him if I was losing it, 'I will tell you to pull your finger out and get on with it. But there's nothing unusual about bawling your eyes out. Have a hot bath, then cry some more if you want to – or go shopping. Now, cup of tea?'

He gently ignored my attempts to create a part-time husband out of him. Offers to arrange his dry-cleaning or have dinner ready for him when he returned to the apartment were rebuffed without insult. His support was very practical. He joined me for lunch when I was restless, prepared dinner, bought ice creams and made tea. We often went out for dinner to the local restaurants on Monday or Tuesday evenings, having pizza in Prahran, then going for a walk, an ice cream and sometimes a visit to the large Borders bookshop where he listened to music while I explored the alternative therapy and spirituality sections for nuggets of advice on grief.

Occasionally at weekends I joined himself and Garry in the mountains for dinner and an evening of music, award shows or other diverting entertainment.

*

It never occurred to me to return to Ireland permanently at this stage. Several people asked the question, usually indirectly – few people asked me anything directly. But my life, my work, my routine, all of my belongings and, of course, Warren and other close friends were in Australia.

The lively social network John and I had established over fourteen years in Australia together disintegrated as soon as he died. When we lived close to Melbourne we had been part of frequent assemblies in Chinatown, St Kilda, Lygon Street or, our favourite, the Vietnamese restaurants in Footscray. This had slowed down when we went to the farm and stopped altogether when he died.

Sometimes I noticed that formerly good social friends had not been in contact since the funeral. I had heard that some people – particularly men – were angry about John's suicide. Others seemed to be avoiding me; perhaps suicide or even death itself were too much to handle in close quarters. Or maybe it had only been John's company they had enjoyed. Or perhaps I was now so out of it that there was no point talking to me at all. Or all of the above.

Or, indeed, none of the above: perhaps it was just a convenient excuse to feel sorry for myself. Our wide network of friends had been terrific around the time of his death, sending me cards, offering help and attending his funeral. Their good wishes were very important collectively. Now I did not have the energy to be social or seek anyone out. I was content to walk on the beach, get a takeaway and sit at home working on our final book together, *River Tracks*, while making friends with television programmes.

My physical contact with anyone other than a masseur or alternative therapists ended when John died. This was hard. John had been a very warm, tactile person; hugging and gentle, passing touches were easy to him. Warren was not into hugging and the brief hugs from friends did not fill the gap. A cat or a dog might have helped but I did not have either. Our cats had died of old age some time before and our dog, Nelson, had died in strange circumstances a few months before John did.

*

Sometimes, often enough in this first year, I dropped into moments of black despair and wished it would all end and I did not care how: nothing could be as bad as this. Suicide now presented itself as an option. I had accepted John's decision; he had shown me it was a way to die, to end all of this suffering. I could make that decision now for myself, end all this awful wailing, isolation and endless self-pity. After eighteen months of John pushing his luck, I had a fair idea of what would work and what would not. Nothing dramatic as a rifle of course: that was a soldier's death – I had heard that from several sources.

'If the bullet has your name on it . . .' John used to say when he mentioned anything about Vietnam. In December 2000 I thought he had run out of bullets but it emerged he had put a small supply in the barn. Sometimes I wondered if he had put his name on one of them.

Deeply depressed and alone, the end would have been a blessed relief. But then a nagging thought would come back to me: 'If I top myself now, I'm only going to have to come back and do all of this grief again. I didn't do it when Mike died so I have to do it now.'

As a result of my scattered reading on grief in the self-help and spirituality books, I had got it into my head that each human life is just one stage of a lengthy, continuous adventure through an unknown world. Consequently, I argued, if I did not deal with my grief and self-pity in this lifetime, it would be waiting for me in the next. And that life might be on a rubbish dump in the Philippines. At least here in Melbourne in 2001, I had loads of advantages. I had all the financial and time resources I needed to get any therapy I wanted, I had access to an excellent collection of professional workers in the field, I had no responsibilities, my work colleagues were tolerant and supportive, I had Warren close by, calm and disengaged, Noeleen and my family were in Ireland, prepared to interrupt their lives to take my phone calls, and close friends in Australia on hand to distract me with walks and lunches. And, at a deep level of consciousness that made me feel strong for a moment, I wanted to see this encounter with grief through to its conclusion, whatever that was. So for me to give up and commit suicide seemed not only bad form but also a complete waste of time and opportunity.

Such arguments, however irrational, were sufficiently motivating to keep me alive for another evening. *Pride and Prejudice*, *Seven Brides for Seven Brothers*, or *An American in Paris* filled the vacuum until I could take a sleeping pill and go to bed.

9

THERAPY

'Have you seen Brenda this week?' Mary asked me on the phone one day.

'Is it that obvious?'

I had not seen my therapist for several weeks and was surprised that Mary could spot this.

'I can hear it in your voice. Cath, I can't stress this enough, you have to see Brenda regularly, preferably every week for the rest of the year. Commit yourself to sessions even if you don't feel the need. This is too much to handle by yourself. You ran away when Mike died, you can't do that again.'

She was right, of course; sibling directness is one of the great gifts of family life. Sixteen years before, when Mike died in the football accident, I had handled my grief very badly. One minute he was alive, a husband with an infant son, next he was dead, gone completely and forever. For a period I drank too much, spent money on rubbish and then charged off like a mad thing to work in the University of Papua New Guinea. Although I was sorely tempted to wrap myself in a black shawl now and do nothing but watch 1950s movies forever, I wasn't dopey enough to think that this way of life was anything more than a fantasy – and ultimately would not suit me anyway. Once more I could hear that voice hidden somewhere inside me urging me along and once more I resolved to manage my grief properly – although I had no idea what that meant. In that inexplicable moment of wisdom and clarity just after John died, I had allocated two years to face the grief full on; for several months I had blundered on in a protective daze and now Mary was the audible voice urging me to take more control.

As a result I established a therapeutic routine with Brenda and soon the practical value of seeing her regularly became clear. The most immediate result was to give me a safe haven in which to download some of the endless conversations that were running through my head at ninety miles an hour. Rather than wear out the people who were closest to me, I learnt to 'park' troubling chatter until I saw Brenda. The power of these one-hour dedicated opportunities to focus on myself was almost physical.

On one occasion, for example, I arrived at a session with the horrible sensation of a hundred thousand boxing matches being fought out under the surface of my skin and a body that ached from head to foot. This had happened quite often outside sessions and was always distressing – I just wanted to jump out of my skin. I usually managed to control the sensation with a fast walk or a couple of Valium but I was interested to see how Brenda would manage it.

Always calm and warm, she tackled the problem immediately, talking quietly: 'Close your eyes, breath deeply.'

A while later she said, 'Now describe what is going on, look at your body.'

Whatever the breathing exercise had done, I was able to look at my body, at the jittery nerves and the boxing matches. Gradually they began to get interesting. I felt the boxing matches going on along my arms and my legs, fighting like lots of little two-person duels just under my skin. As I became more focussed, they began to ease. I was now in no hurry for them to vanish, they had taken on a life of their own and were curious. Soon they were gone – and so was the aching. There was no way I could have calmed down sufficiently to do that exercise at home but when the boxing matches happened next, my attitude had changed: I watched them briefly with wonderment about the impact of grief, then took a Valium or went for a walk.

*

When I was not completely wired, Brenda was in a position to widen the scope of the work and tackle some of my more unstable emotional responses. One of the most significant impacts of grief was my extreme reaction to fairly ordinary, everyday encounters. If someone upset me or annoyed me, I got very upset or very annoyed – not that they would have noticed because I internalised it. Situations and encounters would spin around in my head, day and night. It was exhausting and no amount of telling myself I was overreacting would still the angry internal conversations. Rather than talk through a particular situation at length, Brenda used various techniques to help me understand what I was doing.

My response to the bank was a good example of overreacting. When I received yet another bizarre letter, my usual response was to ring to have the matter sorted out. In normal circumstances that, of course, would have been the end of it but each time, fed by grief, I would not let the story go and would let it replay in my head over and over again. Using deceptively simple techniques, Brenda first helped me to accept without question that the arguments running around my head were my problem and not the bank staff's problem: the bank staff had moved on to other customers and the only person still concerned about the story was me.

'But I didn't create the situation,' I would argue. 'I have spoken to them repeatedly, and sent copies of the death cert and the will to several different sections of the bank; it is the bank people who are so incompetent that their basic communication systems don't work properly. And,' I would usually add crossly, 'they should teach their staff how to handle bereaved people or they'll lose clients.'

From this outraged rant, Brenda would steer me through a process that helped me understand that it was not the bank's job to worry about the emotional fragility of their clients, nor was it my business to worry about whether the bank lost customers because of their inability to handle bereaved people sensitively. My reactions were entirely my choice and therefore my concern only. If I chose to continue to fret, that was my business; if the bank chose to lose customers, that was their business.

Sometimes it would only take me ten minutes to get this point of clarity about whatever was bothering me, sometimes it could take the full hour: 'So if someone is being difficult or carrying on or whatever in my direction, how I react is entirely within my power,' it would eventually click. 'A bank staff member or a colleague or a tram inspector or whoever can stand on their hands shouting at me if they want to; whether I buy into the drama is entirely my choice.'

Each time I would pause to consider the revelation. Each time I would wonder why it had taken me so long to understand something so basic. Each time I would leave the session feeling buoyant and free of worry and chatter. And each time I would find something new to be upset about. In the first couple of years of grief, the knowledge that it was my choice to overreact did not stop me overreacting but at least if I was calm enough, I could understand what was going on and register in the back of my mind that there was an element of choice in it. In addition the pause between feeling buoyant and the start-up of the aggravating chatter lengthened as time went on.

*

This was just part one of the process. Undoubtedly my over-reactions would ease with time – that had happened after Mike died – but the root source of my reaction could be sitting there waiting to erupt the next time I was bereaved or distraught. The regular therapy with Brenda presented me with the opportunity to address root causes properly and forever. It meant looking closely at the emotions that were feeding the responses. Brenda's skill and my complete lack of intellectual resistance allowed me to go into an area that would have had me running for cover in the past; despite my respect for how much therapy was helping me, I still had plenty of residual cynicism about the tedium and implied neurosis of 'going back to your childhood'. Fortunately such cynicism could not get any foothold in my addled brain. Besides, the speed with which Brenda's techniques got to the core of a problem using visualisation and guided meditation made the process interesting.

Brenda explained: 'In the past, usually in early childhood, when we found ourselves in situations that prompted emotions we didn't want to feel, we learnt ways of avoiding those emotions. As a result when something prompts similar emotions in adulthood, this old learnt response kicks in first so we don't even give ourselves the opportunity to feel the contemporary emotions properly.'

That still did not explain the value of excavating old stuff.

'By allowing old, unresolved emotions a chance to be expressed through these meditations,' continued Brenda, 'you are releasing them and letting go any related learnt responses. As you release the old stuff and let go more of these learnt responses, you will be able to respond naturally to current situations.'

*

The practical implications of therapy with Brenda were immense. The most immediate result was that I accepted that endless drawn-out conversations and mental arguments were my business regardless of how they started. Although the chatter in my head continued unabated for quite some time, I now had hope that one day I could stop it. Letting go of my overreactions was much more complex and required a lot of therapeutic guidance but at least when I went to a session with Brenda we could now move quickly into the exercise and chip away at what I now imagined was a deep pile of obsolete, distressed emotions. Each time I experienced those brief moments of calm in Brenda's office, it fed my belief that there was a real, long-term value in doing grief properly.

'If I deal with my grief thoroughly,' I thought repeatedly, 'I will ultimately be able to achieve a much more tranquil life.' I had experienced moments of deep tranquillity during sessions with Brenda. 'Two years,' I said. 'Give it time. Time and trust.'

Once again I appreciated my isolated circumstances, which accommodated this high degree of self-absorption. Warren, the person who would have heard more about this than most, fortunately was curious about the process and listened with interest to the latest update. This was usually three or four days later so I had had plenty of time to make sense of it first.

10

DESERT TRAVELS

Working on our second travel book, *River Tracks*, gave my silent weekends a practical focus and, happily, brought John back into my life. At the time I could not even conjure up his face but when I worked on *River Tracks* I was able to imagine that I was back in the desert where we had spent so much good time together.

In 1998 we had written *Desert Tracks*, a book of desert travel. It had arisen out of our passion for spending time in outback Australia and my own published work on the history of Australian zoos. The publisher had invited us to do a sequel, *River Tracks*. The book was to follow six major rivers from their source to where they met the ocean or another river. Our guidebook provided practical and historical information on how to make each of these rivers a holiday in itself. We had driven most of the rivers together and had been surprised at how much they had offered as integrated holidays in their own right. John had written most of the fishing and survival draft before he died.

I had to drive along parts of several rivers to complete the research, then finish the text and write up the historical sections on Aboriginal, station, communication, railway, paddle steamer and other topics as quickly as possible. If I left it too long, it would become difficult to leave his name on the book but working on *River Tracks* was a good distraction and made it easy for me to fantasise myself out of the black hole for brief periods.

*

Our frequent trips to the desert had been our happiest times together. The desert landscape seemed to absorb John's troubles and he had been at his most peaceful there. In 1988, a year after arriving in Australia from Papua New Guinea, we went into the desert. John had spent a lot of time with the army on exercises in the outback and was confident of his survival skills but our first trip took us into country he did not know at all: the far north of South Australia and western Queensland, areas that look virtually blank on the map.

We set off north from Melbourne with my sister Brigie. I had no idea what to expect but was working on the delusion that at some point we would drive over a ridge and behold a panoramic view of the rolling red dunes of Australia. Instead, after 400 km of farmland, the highway ran through a belt of low dunes and we could discern red sand under the low Mallee trees that spread out either side of the road. Eventually, the ground flattened and a landscape of green scrub stretched out to the horizon. It was broken only by the odd hill here and there, and the occasional dry creek line, identifiable by a row of trees in the middle of nowhere. The further north we moved, the redder and more sparsely covered the ground became. There had been some rain in the region and the landscape was sprinkled with wild flowers. The rain had also left large puddles of water on the track in places and there was danger of the car becoming bogged down in a deceptively deep puddle. The continuous stretch of bitumen had ended in Broken Hill, 800 km north of Melbourne; now we were travelling on dirt or gravel tracks. There was no sign of any other people.

'If we get bogged or the road is too slippy for us to travel on, we'll stay by the vehicle and the track will dry out sooner or later,' John assured us confidently. 'We have plenty of water and food.'

The terrain altered again and as we approached the border between New South Wales, Queensland and South Australia, the red, sandy track ran over high dunes like a roller coaster. Periodically John would stop without warning to point out a lizard, kangaroo or wedge-tailed eagle. As we got closer to our destination, Cooper Creek, 1,550 km north of Melbourne, the terrain flattened and the track shifted in colour from red to the pale grey characteristic of a river bed in this region. The creek was an unexpected sight and far more substantial than the name suggests. At the place John chose as a campsite, the creek was wide and deep and stretched in either direction as far as the eye could see. This was far more than an oasis, it was like a vast inland lake.

The natural environment was blissful. The dry, silent air was broken only the varied sounds of the birds that filled the trees. Flocks of native budgies, white curellas, crows and pelicans moved around, each with their own noises and distinctive behaviours. The curellas – white and yellow birds that look and sound like parrots – woke us at dawn as they squawked loudly from tree to tree. They settled down during the day, usually sitting in pairs on branches in the gum trees.

'They mate for life and live for a long time,' John told us. 'When one of the pair dies, the other pines away.' It was sad to see a single curella sitting alone on the branch of a tree. At sunset the curellas spent another forty-five minutes moving from tree to tree making a deafening racket before settling down for the night. Sometimes we would hear a single, plaintive squawk in the darkness but most of the time there wasn't a sound.

Sunsets across the flat plains were always memorable.

'Come on, girls, the sun is setting, time for a toast,' John invented his own evening ceremony. 'We'll do this properly with malt.'

He loved mature malt and always travelled in the desert with a bottle to toast the sun. Neither Brigie nor I drank whisky.

'It's not whisky, it's an eighteen-year-old malt, it's smooth, smoky and delicious,' he would say as he measured a tiny drop of the precious liquid so that we could toast the sun. 'Here you go, just a capful, don't want you getting used to it.' There was little danger of that but we joined him in thanking the day for bringing us to such a beautiful place without getting bogged on the wet road, stung or bitten.

Then it was time for him to put on a show with one of his lavish campfire dinners. Over the years he baked whole fish and vegetables underground and made perfect bread in a camp oven after proving the yeast on the car bonnet; he made beef stews with freshly baked dumplings, created roast dinners with Yorkshire puds and sauces that would make any restaurant proud, served uncooked fresh fish with wasabi and soya sauce, baked or fried fish that he had caught at dawn for breakfast, and marinated chicken wings and other barbecued meats. Cooking food in a camp for me, my sisters, his brother and friends on our many desert trips was one of the joys in John's life and he always performed with great gestures for his appreciative audience.

At night we slept out under the stars, throwing a tarpaulin, mattresses and lots of pillows on the ground where, according to John, we would be assured of splendid views of sunrise.

*

That first trip to Cooper Creek nearly ended in disaster. One of the features of this desert region is the number of unmarked tracks that run off the official track, including station tracks, tracks around rough parts of the official track and the well-maintained tracks made by the oil and gas mining company. None of these tracks were on any of the standard maps. At times the official track was impossible to identify while a good quality, unmarked track ran close to it before taking off in the wrong direction. It was very easy to take the wrong track – and on this occasion we did, taking ourselves about 70 km out of our way.

We found ourselves having to go across country, hoping that rough unmarked tracks would eventually lead us back to one of the mapped tracks. We were heading for Tibooburra, the nearest town and 370 km from Innamincka and our maps were inadequate for cross-country driving. We still had plenty of food and water but the main danger was running out of petrol. People died in the outback because they ran out of fuel and were not on a major track. John was not concerned. He was confident of his outback survival skills; he also knew our limits.

'We'll keep going until we get close to the point of no return,' he said. 'As soon as we hit the halfway mark with our fuel, we'll turn back to Innamincka. We're not taking any risks.'

About 90 km from Innamincka we drove through what looked like a puddle of water but which turned out to be a very deep hole. We had been through many similar-looking puddles without difficulty so this one was a shock because the water hid an enormous pit. Seconds later we were bogged up to our axle and the water was coming in through the bottom of the car door. As we prepared for the lengthy process of digging ourselves out, a large grader used to maintain the tracks in the area appeared on a track to the south. It was the first vehicle of any description we had seen for nearly 80 km.

'Mate, you found my hole!' he called over the noise of the grader lumbering slowly towards us. 'Made it yesterday, we had great fun trying to get this beauty out of there, it just kept sinking.' The grader resembled a large earth-mover, which explained the unusual size of the hole. Within minutes, he had winched us out and given us directions to get to Tibooburra. 'You're on the right track,' he said cheerfully. 'With all the rain recently, lots more tracks have been created to get around the wet. Just keep going and you'll get there.' Then he faded slowly into the distance like a cumbersome, mythical creature.

We drove on for a number of hours. It was very slow going: the surface of the track was sticky in some places, like ice in others, and at times completely flooded. Fortunately John's driving skills were well able to deal with it. We stopped for the night. Next day we were getting close to our point of no return when John called a halt.

'We'll wait here and see if someone comes along,' he announced. 'We need to confirm we are going in the right direction before going any further. If no one appears, we will have to go back to Innamincka.'

From my perspective this seemed optimistic on two

counts. Since leaving Innamincka two days before, we had only met the grader. In addition we had taken so many unmarked tracks, would we be able to find our way back? But John remained confident. This was what outback adventure was about: knowing the limits and staying cool.

'The most useful survival kit in the desert,' he said cheerfully, 'is a pack of cards. Take them out, start playing patience and sure as anything there'll be some bugger along to tell you to move the red nine onto the black ten.'

This time we did not even have to take out the pack of cards. Minutes after we stopped a white panel van shot out of a track to the south and continued back along the track we had just been on. He had not seen us. John charged after him. The panel van was covered in blood and had scores of dead rabbits swinging off it. John beeped and flashed but was ignored. At a widening of the track he managed to pull alongside the van and I leaned out and shouted, asking the driver if he wouldn't mind pulling over for a minute.

The driver, a man with a long beard, was clearly startled. He stopped and leapt out of his car.

'Have I lost any rabbits?' he demanded.

'No, not that we noticed,' replied John.

'Then what the wanted bloody hell do you want?' he snapped.

He was a rabbit hunter, his car had rolled some time before and he had no windscreen, no rear mirror and was using a spanner for a steering wheel.

'Are we on the right road to Tibooburra?' I asked.

'Yes but you're going in the wrong bloody direction', he said. 'Stay on the track, don't mind the diversions – there are lots of those – and you'll be in Tibooburra without a bother.' He got back into his car and drove off as I was thanking him.

We pushed on and sure enough met a rough red road going south that was actually on the map. Not long afterwards, with only 28-km worth of fuel in the tank, we arrived in Tibooburra.

'No worries,' John announced as if the whole thing had been planned, 'Always knew we would make it. Now how about a gin and tonic?'

*

After that first trip we took every opportunity to spend time in the desert in central Australia. We went across the Simpson several times, down a 2,000-km track through the desert in Western Australia called the Canning Stock Route, up the Oodnadatta Track by the abandoned Ghan railway, up the once notorious Birdsville Track, and to Innamincka and Cooper Creek as often as possible. Sometimes we went alone, sometimes we travelled in a convoy of two or three vehicles, and often we brought friends or family out with us in our vehicle.

John was at home in the desert. Within several hundred kilometres of Melbourne he would open a light beer and relax completely. He enjoyed driving and could continue for a thousand kilometres in a day with me giving him a break for only a hundred kilometres or so. Once we had arrived at a place like Cooper Creek, he would set up his fishing lines and just sit by the water in a camp chair with cool-box full of beer close by. He was a skilled fisherman and there were plenty of fish in the creek. In the early mornings and at dusk John usually caught as many fish as we could eat. The rest of the time he would watch the turtles poking their noses up from the silt-coloured water, the curellas sitting beside their long-term mates on the branches, the budgies chucking each other out of their nests and the pelicans looking for fish, then he would read or doze off under the shade of his hat.

Now I wondered if the total peace he felt by the creek was the same as I had felt sitting on the veranda watching the butterflies. Interrupt it with anything and life becomes stressful again. Interrupt it on a daily basis by having to communicate and interact with people and the stress remains constant. Perhaps that was what he was feeling by the late 1990s when he began to react badly to living in Melbourne. Yet sometimes when he was by the creek I caught him looking into the middle distance, his eyes very far away as they had been that evening on the yacht in Indonesia, and his body tense. In those moments there seemed to be great weight of sadness around him and I wanted to rescue him but he was too far out of reach. I never quizzed him about those times: they were intensely private to him.

Nevertheless I believed that the peace he found in the desert far outweighed his sadness and this was why we had moved to the farm. 'If he can find a place where he could be as calm and peaceful on a daily basis as he is in the desert,' I reasoned, 'perhaps that will help him.' For me that hope was enough to override the inconvenience of living so far from our lives in Melbourne.

It didn't work, but at least we had given it a go.

11

JOHN'S LAST MONTH

In the immediate aftermath of John's death and my descent into self-absorbed grief, I had not thought much about the impact his suicide might have had on my family in Ireland. Although Australia was very far away and the events leading up to John's death were just as remote, my family and friends loved John also. My mother had visited us in Papua New Guinea, three of my sisters had visited us in Australia more than once and we had visited Ireland together several times. John's personality and gregarious manner had won everyone over. When his mother died in 1997, he had flown over to the funeral in England and gone on to Ireland with his brother where everyone made them both welcome. He had enjoyed belonging to a warm, extended family, and said so more than once. He was also my husband and in that context, I felt it was important that my family should have no unanswered questions about his death.

By May I had the energy to go to Ireland and bring some closure for them on the immediacy of John's death. Although the bank saga continued, the administration had eased off a bit so I could leave it for a few weeks. The throbbing in my head, the boxing matches under my skin, the jumpiness and the sleepless nights, however, were ongoing and relentless so sitting squashed in a plane for twenty-four hours was not an option, as it could have driven me over the edge. Using the War Widow's pension, I upgraded to business class, which seemed to be an outrageous expense but a psychological necessity.

In fact it turned out to be an excellent experience in the circumstances. For twenty-four hours I had people around me who wanted to ensure I was comfortable, brought me tea and periodically asked me if everything was OK. I felt pathetically pleased by this but after six months of looking after myself, it was a treat. The airline I flew with also provided a free limousine service for business-class travellers so it meant that I would be driven to the airport and picked up when I returned. John had always driven me to the airport if I was going somewhere alone, and stayed with me at the entrance to departures as if he would never see me again. Now the airport would be soulless so the limo service compensated well enough.

*

Once in Ireland it was strange being in so much company again. It was early summer, the weather was pleasant and I sat in gardens or walked in the Dublin Mountains telling the story of the build-up to John's death. They had all heard snippets about how John had not been well during the last eighteen months of his life. They knew he had had a rough childhood; they also knew that he periodically woke me with his nightmares about Vietnam. Two of my sisters who had come to the desert with us had seen him in very melancholy mood there and a third sister who had visited the farm had seen how distressed he was becoming. Now I wanted them all to have as much information as they wished about the lead-up to his death so that they could be as accepting about his decision as I was.

Telling the story and answering questions was not stressful. I usually began the story the night before my birthday in November 2000 when John said he would shoot himself if I didn't give him the bottle of vodka that he had bought me as a present.

*

My birthday that year was on the first Sunday in November. On the Friday before, John had worked from home. When I had arrived at the farm in the evening, I found him slumped on the veranda; his responses were exceptionally slurred. If I had seen an empty whisky bottle beside him, I would not have been surprised at his condition but the only alcohol visible was a bottle of wine with a single glass taken out of it. Therefore I thought he had had a stroke and was about to call an ambulance when he began to snore. John had not had any spirits for the previous two months, wine and beer had never affected him like this before and he had never hidden his drinking, so I could not work out what was causing this condition. Later I found a bulky shop receipt indicating that he had bought a bottle of whisky and a bottle of vodka.

Next morning he grinned cheekily, as he usually did when he had taken something that was bad for his body. He had adult-onset diabetes and was supposed to control it by diet but he could never resist food or drinks that were bad for him. Usually it was chocolate or cake or something full of sugar. Now it looked like he had drunk a bottle of whisky but I did not ask and he did not offer the information.

'I got you vodka for your birthday,' he said producing the bottle from a cupboard.

'Thanks, love,' I seldom drank vodka but was not going to let that detail interfere now. 'I'll put it away until I want it.' He spent the day working apparently content-edly in the vegetable garden while I worked on *River Tracks*. That evening he had a mood swing and asked me for the vodka.

'No love, it's mine, you gave it to me, I've put it away.' For some time spirit consumption had tended to precede his most pronounced mood swings and, during a two-month abstinence, the swings had eased a bit. The idea of him starting to drink spirits again was very troubling. 'There is wine in the barn and there's beer in the fridge if you're desperate.'

His mood got worse but despite his demands something stopped me from giving him the vodka. He left the house angrily. It was dark but warm. Ten minutes later he reappeared on the veranda carrying his rifle. He paced up and down for a while, the wide glass doors open.

'If you don't give me the vodka,' he said holding the rifle, 'I'll shoot myself.'

I tried to reason with him, as I had done on previous occasions but felt that if I gave him the vodka, I would be making the decision as to whether he would live or die. I could not do it and subconsciously locked into place on this, refusing to give him the vodka and telling him that any decision had to be his own.

He vanished. I rang my sister Mary in Ireland. It was Saturday morning in Ireland and she was not there. I rang my sister Sheila and told her what was happening, oblivious to the fact that she was standing in her hallway with two small children about to leave the house for a day of busy activity. As Sheila was talking to me, I heard a sound and asked her to hang on while I went out into the darkness. John was sitting on the front veranda, holding the rifle close and staring into the distance. He did not answer me but at least he was still alive.

He came back into the house a short while later. 'I didn't kill myself because it's too close to your birthday and I don't want your birthday to be associated with this.' Then he went to bed and fell asleep.

My birthday next day was peaceful. He was very attentive and set up a feast of interesting food and boutique wine, just as he would have done in the past. We were both too exhausted to talk about the previous night's events so we allowed the day to move through as a gentle indulgence. On Tuesday, however, he apologised for the scene on Saturday. It was a bank holiday – Melbourne Cup Day – and we were in the orchard; the weather was warm, the air silent and the butterflies were flitting about. 'I know now it was not your business,' he said. 'You were right, it is my decision and I'm really very sorry for putting you through that, I should never have done that to you.'

For the second time in over a year of flirting with suicide, he had apologised for what he was putting me through. However this was the first time he had acknowledged that whether he went on living or killed himself was his decision alone.

The next four weeks were a nightmare. He went out to the paddocks on several occasions and let off the rifle. The shots echoed through the valleys. It was a high-powered firearm that he kept to shoot sheep, deer and other large animals in trouble. When he had lived in the Northern Territory before I met him, he had been a keen hunter. He was an excellent shot; in the army he said he was a military 'class one' shot. In target practice on the farm, he demonstrated he had not lost it, hitting the target accurately between 93 per cent and 97 per cent of the time. In recent years he abhorred the idea of killing any animal for pleasure but several times he had had to put a sick sheep down and it had caused him terrible anguish. The rifle was at least a humane source of death for sick animals.

Each time I heard the rifle shot during that month, I wondered what I would find if I went out to look. Each time he came back to the house looking weighed down with deep troubles but was usually uncommunicative.

His liver doctor was concerned about his overall state of mind and suggested he go in for an alcohol detox, which involved therapy and other processes. Sadly the detox was an unmitigated disaster. John swapped alcohol for sleeping pills and tranquillisers and came home with a large supply of both. There he mixed the tranquillisers with alcohol, creating more trouble. His liver doctor was away, his psychiatrist had rejected my intervention on a previous occasion, so I rang the detox doctor hoping for help. I got his assistant.

'We have fifty to a hundred patients,' he told me, sounding horribly officious. 'We can't chase them all up. Anyway it is none of your business. If the patient feels he has a problem he can ring us. I am not at liberty to discuss the patient's situation with you.'

No amount of reasoning about how deeply illogical that argument was or pleading to his humanity would change his mind. I had just had a crash course in the bureaucracy involved in dealing with mental illness where there is apparently no role for an adult patient's immediate family. I did not want to barge in on John's autonomy but at the same time he was sitting up on a mountain eating pills, drinking alcohol, threatening suicide and being silent for a lot of the time. I was running out of options. For moments during the day, he was still there, chatty and loving, but much of the time he was silent, sitting deep within himself and unapproachable except when he was asleep and crying and then he held on to me tightly. I didn't sleep much during this period.

However, the drums were beating and John's veteran mates realised there was a problem. Paul, his Veteran Association's welfare officer, persuaded John to attend a special two-week residential therapy process especially designed for Vietnam veterans. He was to start on Friday 8 December. On Wednesday, two days before, John decided to check whether he could use his Veterans' Gold Card to attend psychotherapy sessions with a therapist he had recently met at the detox clinic. He had liked her and, perhaps because I had had a few sessions with Brenda, he was prepared to try out this approach to helping himself. The Gold Card entitled him to free medical treatment but claiming psychotherapy required authorisation in advance.

He was on the phone to Veterans Affairs for thirty minutes – as the phone bill later indicated. During the course of conversation, he must have said that he was suicidal. Knowing John it was probably accompanied by a comment like, 'and it's none of your business. Just tell me if I can use the card or not.' The upshot of that conversation was that the counsellors in Veterans Affairs informed our local police station that there was a suicidal veteran with a rifle in their precinct. The police sergeant rang John and then rang me at work.

'We've been informed that your husband is suicidal and has a firearm,' he said. 'I have spoken to him and he has threatened to kill us if we go near him.'

'He would never do that,' I protested. 'He is a very law-abiding person and has the utmost respect for the police.'

'I have to inform you that he said if we tried to get the rifle off him that he would shoot at us.'

Yes, he probably had said that because he would have hated the interference. As well as that I was beginning to wonder where his mind was. Recently he had taken to flicking into a mood that I had only ever seen previously on Anzac Day, Australia's annual day of commemoration for war veterans. When he was in that mood, he would become unpredictable, his facial expression and his eyes would harden and his voice would become cold and distant. Without warning, his responses to me or to someone else present could turn angry and intractable. Was that the mood he was in now?

I became concerned for the safety of the police. 'John is an excellent shot,' I said to the police officer. 'He has sights on his rifle and will see you coming around the mountain. There is no one else at the house and I can get the rifle off him when he is asleep.' The idea of sneaking John's rifle out of the house was abhorrent to me but the idea of the police forcibly taking the rifle off John and possibly even sectioning him was worse.

'You know that when someone threatens to kill themselves like this, they usually do,' the sergeant added unnecessarily. 'I'll decide later whether to approach him or not.'

I could not get hold of John by phone. I was in Melbourne and at least two hours from the property but it could be risky going there now. I did not know what to expect. Then John rang. He was wired, looking out for danger and jumping at the slightest sound. He definitely seemed to be in that unpredictable Anzac Day mood, although I had never heard him as bad as this before. He sounded like he was calling from a war zone, talking quietly, going silent, reporting 'all clear', going silent again, then getting angry about being under threat of intruders on his own property. Without warning his voice returned to a normal tone and he said he was going to make phone calls and would talk to me later.

An hour later I rang. He was cross with the police for stirring up trouble. 'It's none of their business, why don't they just leave me alone.' There was a faraway tone in his voice and he sounded weary. My heart went out to him but I had to decide whether to go home to the mountains or not. I had planned to stay in the town apartment that night and had about ten minutes to decide whether to dash for the last train or go home first thing in the morning. This was probably the hardest decision of my life and to this day I am not sure whether I made the correct one or not. I decided to stay in town and be home by 9 a.m. the following morning. Part of me was concerned for the first time ever about danger from John and wanted him to settle down before I arrived, part of me wanted to rush home and hold him like I had done several times in the previous weeks, and part of me was just plain dog-tired and unable to face the long trip on the train and up the mountain.

John was calm on the phone that evening. Paul had been in touch and confirmed the place at the Veterans' therapy clinic on Friday. Paul also spoke to me and explained why Veterans Affairs had had to call the police and why the police reacted as they did. 'Everyone had to do their jobs according to tried and tested processes; lives, particularly of family members, have been saved that way in the past.' I was hopeful about Friday.

When I arrived home at 9 a.m. on Thursday morning, John was pottering about the house and garden. He looked terribly tired and worn out but was otherwise quiet. There was no sign of the anger or paranoia from the previous day. We meandered around the farm, collecting eggs, looking at progress in the vegetable garden and chatting. That was when he said he wanted his ashes scattered on the Long Paddock on our property.

After lunch he sat outside. He could barely lift his eyes to look at me. I held him; his body was so tense it was hard and unyielding. I tried to be optimistic about the therapy starting the next day, saying there was hope and that it didn't have to be like this. He did not seem to hear anything. He sat with his head down between his shoulders. His movements were slow and there was very little life left in his eyes.

I drove to town to get comfort food of the type he shouldn't be eating. If the therapy worked, he would not be eating this sort of food in the future.

At about 6.30 p.m. that evening I was preparing dinner and he stood at the sliding door of the veranda with the rifle. We had a brief conversation, I started to prepare dinner and he walked off to the barn slowly and sadly, dragging the butt of the rifle on the ground.

12

TALKING TO JOHN

When I was in Ireland on this first trip back after John's death, I visited Maria. The last time I had spoken to her was the morning after John died. The conversation had helped immeasurably; I don't know if I would ever have achieved the same degree of peace about John's death without her input. Now I was going to see her with no expectation other than a calming session of alternative therapy.

'He's here,' she said, smiling at an empty space in front of her.

I knew from her expression that she was certainly responding to someone with John's flirtatious character. He had always enjoyed the company of women and chatted easily to them. In Melbourne he used to have endless conversations with women of all ages who passed our house while he was gardening. At Australian Army barbecues where women sat at tables on the grass and the men swung out of the veranda drinking beer, John always plonked himself among the women. And no woman ever left our house without a bear hug and a large rose from the front garden.

Maria was very relaxed with the presence of John's spirit. I did not know what to say or how to react although it felt very natural that John should be there. 'Is he all right?'

'Oh yes, he's much lighter now. He has a huge spirit; he's very evolved and in his lifetime he touched everyone he met.'

'Was there anything else I could have done?' If there was any reality in this, I might as well take advantage of it and ask the burning question because at times I had responded badly to his mood swings. If he had had a diagnosable illness and I had known he was about to die, I might have been more patient. Not long after his death, a friend had asked me if I felt guilty. I did not understand what she had been talking about then: guilty about what? I had felt no responsibility for John's death and there was no doubt in my mind but that it had been entirely his decision. At the same time I wondered if I could have done things differently somewhere along the line.

Maria paused.

'You're asking that question because you felt that John felt you could have resolved some of his great problems. Even after he died, you still felt that you could have solved some of his problems. But just before he died, he realised that he had to solve his own problems.'

Yes, that made sense. It also fitted in with my reaction on the night of the vodka incident. That had seemed to be the beginning of the end.

'And no,' continued Maria in her matter-of-fact way. 'No, there was nothing else you could have done. You were marvellous and did masses as it was.'

I accepted that. It was what I wanted – and needed – to hear, although part of me had already known the answer to that question. I lay down on the massage bed and Maria gave me a healing, using signs, evoking saints and touching my feet. I had no idea what she was doing but it definitely helped me to feel more relaxed than I had been in a long time. It did not bother me that the sensation would probably only last as far as the bus stop because every good sensation was worth savouring when it happened.

Just before I left, Maria asked, 'Do you ever speak to John?'

It was an insightful question because it had been a source of anxiety that I had not been able to see or hear him much since I left the farm.

'I don't know how to,' I answered. 'I've tried but I can't seem to see him. I don't know how to talk to him.'

Maria smiled. 'Well, he wants to talk to you. Talk about the weather, talk about anything, just talk to him.'

'But is that fair? I don't want to drag him back from wherever he is and force him to hang around earth again.'

The odd assortment of books I had read after John died had included the *Tibetan Book of Living and Dying* and other books incorporating Buddhist teachings. From the snippets I had read, I had put together the idea that the spirit disconnects from the body and moves into a new realm. I would never pass an exam on Buddhist concepts of living and dying but I found it easy to believe that John was out there somewhere; I also believed I should not be bothering him in whatever constituted an afterlife.

'Well, he's around and he wants you to talk to him.'

She suggested I get rune stones with a book of interpretations by Ralph Blum.

'Pick one of the stones and check what it means in Blum's book. Each one has a symbol, a name and an interpretation. You can also ask John questions, then pick a rune stone and read what it is about.'

It all sounded a bit strange. How could John make me pick a particular rune stone from a bag containing twenty-five stones? And how could a 200-word interpretation be a meaningful communication between my dead husband and me. The bookshop Hodges Figgis in Dawson Street had the book Maria recommended – in fact it had quite a large collection of similar material. The book came with twenty-five smooth, marked stones in a red velvet bag. I returned to Australia with yet another way of getting through each day.

13

THE SPIRITUAL DIMENSION

Flying back into Melbourne, I was very glad that an airline employee met me with a sign and a car. Warren had left the heat on so the flat was warm but deadly silent. The mail sat in a neat pile. I opened anything that was not from the bank. Sitting in the middle of the usual stuff was a review of an American book on the history of zoos. It was a compilation of essays about zoos all over the world written by an international who's who of zoo historians. I had written the Australian chapter and felt it an honour to be in such company. The lengthy review singled out my chapter for special mention and devoted a chunky section of the review to saying how good it was. I was thrilled and rang my father in Ireland, knowing how delighted he would be. The wobbly return was over.

Now my weeks settled into a pattern. I finished *River Tracks*, increased my working week to four days and saw Brenda on a weekly basis. Warren was around on Mondays, Tuesdays and sometimes Wednesdays; the rest of the time I was alone. I walked, had baths, read Jilly Cooper and other airport novels by women, watched TV, worked my way through the substantial old-movie section in the local video store and arranged flowers.

Two friends took me out to a nearby Indian restaurant. John was dead seven months and this was the first time I was in a social situation that should have included him. I could feel some panic rising and did not want to go but went in the end. It was pleasant but I found social conversation such an effort that I was in no hurry to repeat the experience. It was much easier to spend the weekends alone.

It was not a particularly lonely time because now I could talk to John. Communicating with the world beyond was very seductive and I used a pendulum to get 'yes' or 'no' answers to questions. Keeping my hand perfectly still, I would ask a question and the pendulum would swing easily in different directions in response. I had no interest in seeking a scientific reason for this. Few people knew of this particular obsession although at first it had seemed so natural that I had not held back from mentioning it to close friends. But after noticing a few expressions that said clearly, 'Oh my God, what is she on?' I shut up, which was probably wise. Between the wailing, isolating myself for three days every week, the woolly connection with work-based activities and total avoidance of anyone I did not know extremely well, adding a belief in conversations with my dead husband would probably be the final straw.

In fact the spiritual element quickly became the most interesting part of my grief. It presented a bigger-picture version of life that was interesting and challenging. For a long time, probably from my teenage years until 1999, spirituality equated with religion for me and so was to be ignored. I was born in 1957 and was raised as an Irish Catholic. Religion was an integral part of my life with major ceremonies livening up the standard commitment of weekly attendance at mass. As the Troubles in the north of Ireland erupted in the late 1960s, the behaviour of people in the name of religion became confusing; and in the 1970s and early 1980s, the bullying behaviour and political involvement of the Irish Church eventually led me to a high degree of cynicism and a suspicion of organised religion. Nevertheless, after sixteen years abroad, I was happy to claim that I was a cultural Catholic. I was familiar with the rich traditions of Christianity; knowledge of the fundamental teachings of the Church informed my general understanding of aspects of other religions and cultures; I was comfortable with concepts of mystery and faith; and I was even comfortable with suffering, as we had been warned from a very early age that everyone would have a cross to bear at some stage in their lives. I appreciated the Catholic Church's important, milestone ceremonies in marking the stages in a person's life publicly; I attended baptisms, confirmations, marriages and funerals with an enthusiastic sense of participation but felt no obligation to buy into Catholic moral dogma nor obey its intrusive rules.

Churches outside mass-time became very peaceful places to go – although the predominance of gory images of Christ dying on the cross was not always conducive to a peaceful contemplation of life and the spirit. I really wanted images of a peaceful Christ or even a Buddha on the altar so I could focus my attention on something that wasn't supposed to scare the living daylights out of me. Consequently I much preferred quiet contemplation in a church with simple statuary or, when I was in Southeast Asia, a Buddhist temple.

My Irish upbringing had also introduced me to the concept of fairies and other spirits around the countryside. My father had woven stories about leprechauns into the landscape around our family holiday base in Roundstone. 'I don't believe in fairies but they're there,' was a phrase I had heard in childhood and accepted with ease. For example I believed it was asking for trouble to build a house on a circle of stones known as a fairy fort and had no hesitation in accepting stories of collapsing extensions or troubled lives that followed construction over one of these stone circles. There were also several believable 'ghost' stories in the recent family history; these involved incidents where something inexplicable and other-worldly had had a positive influence on a situation.

Warren had sparked off my interest in non-specific spirituality in 1999. He was dealing with a health issue and Vince, his naturopath, began to incorporate a spiritual dimension into the otherwise highly practical treatment. One evening Warren asked me in conversation whether I believed in God or anything 'out there'. I had looked out at the sky and without thinking too much about it said, 'Well, I never believed that Mike had actually vanished to nothing. He's out there somewhere but I have no idea what that means.'

I began to pay attention to Warren's own pursuit of spiritual matters. He had close connections to an inclusive Anglican Church in the country where he played the organ on Sundays and on Christmas Eve. He did not have a negative history with a church to make him wary like so many Irish people of my generation.

'Vince suggested I say the Lord's Prayer,' he said after a visit to the naturopath. 'He said that, given the number of people in the world who would be saying it at any particular time, it has power. I have always liked that prayer and would say it in times of need anyway. I find it comforting, probably because it's so well known and easy to say and flows so nicely. You could try it, see if it works.'

Vince also suggested books to Warren, many of which had a Buddhist element to them. The concepts and sentiments were appealing but, having survived life under one belief system, I was not about to subscribe to another. Besides after so many years abroad, I appreciated being a cultural Catholic. I could draw on the elements of the Catholic Church's belief systems that seemed pure. And of course I could also draw on pure elements of other religions' teachings that appealed to me. It was an eclectic mix that supported peace of mind. And it was easy to do in Australia where no one made a fuss about religion or spirituality so long as it wasn't too obvious and didn't interfere with anyone else.

*

But by having conversations with a dead person, asking him questions and taking the swing of a pendulum as a direct answer, was I moving beyond the already liberal bounds of Australian eclecticism into a degree of craziness? In a strange way, it was one of the advantages of being so isolated. Warren, who was probably closest to me during this time, maintained a level of curiosity but never interfered or judged. Swinging pendulums and talking to John did not bother him one way or the other. Besides, I thought, if I was determined to give so much energy to grief, I might as well push the boundaries.

However, in Ireland Noeleen was on my case and, after several phone conversations on the subject, stepped in. 'Cath, it's time to stop taking the pendulum literally. You are using it too much. Keep picking runes and reading the interpretations, they seem to be working well for you but just chat to John. Don't ask him direct questions and don't look for answers. This is a very difficult time for you and you'll hold on to anything, so just go easy for the moment. This time will pass.'

I pulled back on taking the pendulum literally but went on chatting with John. I talked to him – without moving my lips – when I was walking through Albert Park, sitting on St Kilda beach watching the sunset, or on lengthy drives in the car.

Once I got caught out. I was on the beach in the dark working through the interminable chatter in my head and drawing John into the discussion. I reached some sort of conclusion and said something out loud. It was pitch dark and there seemed to be no one around. The waves on the shore disguised the noise of the nearby road and cafes. The only thing that could hear me talking to myself was the heap of seaweed in front of me. Suddenly the heap of seaweed moved and a man sat up, took a swig out of a bottle and started talking to himself. It was so dark that he possibly did not see me although I was only a few feet away. He had probably heard me talking and had woken up. So there we were, two dotty people talking to themselves on the beach – it seemed perfectly normal for the colourful suburb of St Kilda. I smiled broadly all the way home – also a behaviour that would not have raised an eyebrow in St Kilda.

14

RETURN TO THE DESERT

Noeleen visited me in Australia when *River Tracks* was finished. We packed up the car and went to the desert together. John had taught me so well that I had enough confidence to drive via the safest route to Cooper Creek and the place on the permanent waterhole where we had always made camp. The British tourist Peter Falconio had vanished along the Stuart Highway north of Alice Springs a month before Noeleen arrived. It was a tragic reminder of the vulnerability of travellers in the outback. I set some guidelines for us by imagining what John might have advised two women who were going into the desert alone.

'We won't stop for anyone. I have the radios and, if we can't talk to the person in difficulty on the UHF, we will alert someone at the next town or station. If anyone asks, don't give any information about our movements. We will be camping away from everyone and can use the darkness as cover.'

'How does that work?'

'When there's little or no moon, it's pitch dark at night in the desert because there's no backlight. The only way anyone can see us is if we are in the light of the campfire or have a camp light shining near us. If anyone bothers us, just move into the darkness and crouch down into the shadow of a shrub. Anyway, where we'll be camping, no one could approach us without using lights so we'll see them coming.' I had no fear about the region to which we were going.

'What about snakes and things?'

'Don't worry about those. I haven't seen many snakes over years of travelling, and when I did it was a privilege.'

Except perhaps that time a lethal tiger snake went around my foot towards the bed, which had been on a tarpaulin on the ground as usual. But there was no point telling Noeleen that story until we got back to Melbourne. We were not taking a tent and I did not want to destroy her sleep.

'We'll stick to tracks that are relatively busy – two or three cars along a track is busy enough to get us out of difficulty. We'll be safe,' I assured her. 'And not just because John will be keeping an eye on us,' I added just in case she thought she was putting her life into the hands of a spaced-out, grieving widow. 'This trip is planned on the best principles of desert safety. Fear not!'

It was wonderful to be in the desert again – even if John was only with us in spirit and memory. The space, the air, that peculiar desert silence, the peace and the beauty were all so welcoming. Each evening, looking out at the moon on the water, or sitting during the day in a landscape with only ourselves in it, I could see why John found so much peace there. The desert could absorb his troubles. Now it was absorbing mine. I wondered if it could absorb any troubles John still had in spirit.

We attracted attention whenever we stopped: two women driving the large, 4.2 litre Land Cruiser, the king of outback vehicles, equipped with bull bar, spotlights, radio aerials and heavy-duty suspension, were bound to cause some minor curiosity. Most tourists in the outback are in male parties, couples or families. Two women travelling by themselves were not a common sight. Fortunately most people approached Noeleen to find out where we were going. She could honestly say, 'I don't know,' by which stage I was back in the car or had vanished into the roadhouse.

We cooked a downsized version of our traditional dinners. Steaming vegetables underground was easy and we even did a roast, but the rest of the time stuck to barbecues.

'You're cheating Noeleen,' I could imagine John saying. 'What about dumplings or a whole fish? At least you could make her a proper roast with Yorkshire puds and a wine sauce.'

'Shut up, Johnson, you're dead. I'm here and in charge. I am not cooking for the next two hours and creating lots of dirty pots.'

I liked encounters with that, even if they were based on memory. It made me smile and made John feel more present. And besides, if he were in spirit watching me creating a dinner for Noeleen without going to all the trouble he would have gone to, that's exactly what he would have said.

*

Three weeks later, Noeleen left Australia. It was now September. John was dead nine months and it was hard to see how my life could ever be normal again. Would I ever be able to sleep through the night? Would I ever stop missing John on a daily basis? Would I ever stop missing the warmth of an intimate relationship? Would my brain always be fudge? Would I always forever jumpy when I met people I didn't know? Would my head ever shut up and give me a moment's peace? Experience told me it was a matter of time; in my state of mind I accepted this and reasoned that whatever got me through was fine. I was in no mood to analyse any potential long-term damage my approach to grief might have; I did not feel altogether sane but I was still working, was eating well enough and taking exercise and had not suffered any noticeable damage, so I maintained my course.

Blum's interpretations of the runes, which Maria had recommended, were soothing, almost like prayers. The 200–350 word interpretation of whichever rune stone I picked seemed to lift me slightly whenever I was feeling low or isolated. Often I would pick one or two just before going to bed. Such was my mental condition that every rune was applicable to how I was feeling.

Perth or *Initiation* included the line, 'Deep inner transformational forces are at work here. Yet what is achieved is not easily or readily shared.' That was an important one; it suggested that something useful was happening while I was in self-imposed isolation. Sometimes I became concerned by my isolation and wondered if I should seek out an evening class or try making new friends; I readily accepted *Perth* as suggesting that it was not necessary yet. *Berkana* or *Growth* incorporated a gentle nudge: 'What is called for here is to consider your issue with care and awareness . . . For this to happen, your will must be clear and controlled.' If, when I first looked at the stone, the symbol was reversed, the message contained a louder nudge: 'You may feel dismay at failing to take right action. But rather than dismay, what is called for here is diligence.' Around this time it was easy to let administrative and work-related tasks slide so I used this rune to inject a bit of energy and focus into my activities and to stop using grief as a way of avoiding action.

A few runes helped me to accept the difficult reality of my situation. *Uruz* or *Strength* reaffirmed my decision to go with everything grief could throw at me; it states:

> *Positive growth and change may involve a descent into darkness as part of the cycle of perpetual renewal. As in nature, this progression consists of five aspects: death, decay, fertilisation, gestation, rebirth. Events occurring now may well prompt you to undergo a death within yourself. And since self-change is never coerced – we are always free to resist – remain mindful that the new form, the new life, is always greater than the old. Prepare, then, for opportunity disguised as loss.*

My favourite rune was *Gebo* or *Partnership*; it always felt like a kiss from John:

> *Drawing this Rune is an indication that partnership in some form is at hand . . . True partnership is achieved only by separate and whole beings who retain their separateness even as they unite. Remember to let the winds of heaven dance between you.*

It appeared frequently – at least I thought it did; it was months before I realised that *Partnership* looked very similar to *Nauthiz* or *Pain*. The interpretation for *Nauthiz* began with 'The necessity of learning to deal with severe constraint is the lesson of *Nauthiz*'. I was probably picking *Nauthiz* as often as *Partnership* but I was glad I had not noticed because *Partnership*'s interpretation would calm any agitation instantly and was therefore a most effective tranquilliser during that time.

Were the runes John's way of talking to me? Did they really contain messages and information about my subconscious progress through grief? Who knows? It didn't really matter because, for a few moments before sleeping, I was happy to believe they were positive, motivational messages from the unknown and that belief brought a moment of warm comfort.

15

HOMEOPATHIC ESCAPADE

My next adventure was quite weird. If it was as real as it seemed to be, it was quite wonderful. If it was not real at all, it was one hell of a story. It began with Vince, my ever-supportive naturopath, who was keeping my body going. I had seen him a couple of times for minor things before John died but now he was an important support to my recovery process. My body was reacting very badly to John's death. Everything from night sweats, a painful digestive system and pain in my lungs to heart palpitations and electric shocks buzzing through my head. My medical doctor organised lots of tests courtesy of the War Widow's Gold Card. But I knew, and my doctor knew, that it was all stress. Medication was not the answer on an ongoing basis. Weekly, private yoga classes helped, as did the occasional relaxing massage. I was also visiting Vince, the naturopath, periodically and his potions and knowledge of Chinese medicine were a critical support. Apparently my yin and yang were out of sync.

'Does your bed feel like concrete?' he asked at one session.

'How did you know? Even my feather pillows seem hard at times. Often it is very difficult to get comfortable in bed.'

'That's a common response to grief and will pass. For the last number of years you have been managing the situation with your late husband. That is using lots of masculine energy or the yang. Now it is time to nurture the yin or feminine energy to bring your energy into balance.'

It turned out that this meant eating fresh food and vegetables, pacing myself, not trying to be in control of every minute, and taking it easy. For me this translated into having baths, not running for trams, eating loads of fish and steamed vegetables, and avoiding alcohol.

One day Vince suggested I take the homeopathic remedy, Ignatia, at its most dense level. 'It is for grief and will help shift things at an energy level.'

I had no idea in practical terms what this meant but I trusted him and was game to try anything that promised to reduce the tension in my body and get my brain working at full capacity again.

'Take it for five weeks. It may be a bit rough at times as you are clearing old stuff but should be worth it in the long run.'

The little bottle of drops looked benign but Brenda was not happy about it when I saw her next. 'That's very powerful stuff, it will knock you about,' she warned.

She contemplated it for a while then agreed that I should continue but suggested that I see Josepha, a kinesiologist, to make sure the homeopathic remedy was tuned into my body and would do what it was supposed to.

*

Kinesiology was new to me; I had no idea what it involved but I trusted Brenda. Financially it was not a problem: I treated the War Widow's pension as money to help with my overall recovery process. I had never asked for or expected that money so it became the resource that allowed me to try alternative ways of regaining peace of mind and a calm body.

The visit to Josepha was a tremendous experience. I lay down and she asked me questions, using the response from my wrist muscles to get an answer.

'This is muscle testing. I'm working with the energy flow in your body and using muscle testing to identify imbalances or blockages; the imbalances can be caused by emotional as well as physical trauma,' explained Jospeha.

She was convincing as she talked. She asked me to move my limbs in certain ways and held my wrist to monitor my response. With minimal input from me, she identified lots of my ongoing physical problems and appeared to be moving energy around my body as if she was putting it back into its rightful place. I enjoyed listening to her.

'Oh, my goodness,' she said suddenly looking up beyond my head. The little bottle of homeopathic remedy was sitting on the chest. 'This remedy isn't for you at all, it's for John. He had some problem with his mother and this remedy is shifting that. Fascinating,' she added to herself.

She was off, talking about John and his mother – I think. She did not need any information from me to produce a general sense of John's relationship with his mother. John indeed had had a difficult relationship with his mother. He adored her but lost her when she turned to alcohol when he was about seven – as far as he remembered. This added to the violence already in the house. John tried to intervene in fights between his parents to protect his mother from his father but as the adults fought, John's efforts only dragged him into the battle. His arm was broken twice, he was knocked unconscious at least once and he often went to school with bruises and black eyes. This prompted kids in the school to pick fights with him.

He told me other stories about the seven years he spent living with two alcoholic parents until he left home at fourteen. 'If you want to know about my life in South Shields', he said once, 'read *Angela's Ashes*. Mc Court pulls his punches but you will get a sense of the poverty and the endless humiliation.' I had heard stories about how his bedclothes had been piles of coats and other clothes, about him going to school with no underwear so he couldn't play sports, about having to rely on free meals at the 'pauper's table' in grammar school, about being sent over to aunts for a bath and food, about being sent to 'uncles' to get money, about dragging his parents home from the pub on Sundays at lunchtime and about pulling up floorboards to burn in the solid-fuel cooker – the list of indignities went on. But it was the memories of his childhood relationship with his mother that had often led to silence and tears. Like Vietnam, these were memories he never wanted to explore and I didn't probe.

'The Ignatia is allowing John to clear stuff through you,' Josepha continued. 'He needs to clear things to do with his mother that he wasn't able to clear when he was alive. If you are happy to go ahead with that, I can help you to take it.'

'Go for it.' It all sounded very strange and a bit kooky but even if I had been aware at the time that Ignatia contains strychnine, I would not have hesitated. If I could have lifted John's troubles when he was alive, I would have done so. Now he was dead, Josepha had given me something oddly practical I could do and I accepted the challenge.

*

The homeopathic experience felt like an adventure into the exotic and the unknown. I had the strangest of dreams. I felt quite weird most of the time, sometimes I felt great, sometimes terrible. My body reacted violently and in unexpected ways at times but never when I was at work. John even appeared in one of my therapy sessions much to Brenda's consternation.

'I don't usually allow this', she said, 'but he is determined to stay, he won't go away.'

She went on working with me, occasionally looking like she was talking to John. I took it for granted he was present in some shape or other. Then, like a mother scolding an errant child, Brenda sent him on his way.

'He's a cheeky one,' Brenda said smiling at him as he vanished – I presume.

*

Warren was curious as usual but also kept a discreet eye on me to make sure that I ate properly and did not go off the rails entirely. Most of the time I was able to function but for that five-week period, there was definitely something going on. All the time I just hoped it was doing whatever it was supposed to be doing. Then the five weeks ended and that adventure was over. I did not get a report card or the all-clear or anything. There was nothing to say that the Ignatia had been successful. It was a weird world to be interfacing with. None of the rules of life seemed to apply but Catholic tradition had made me comfortable with the idea that the souls of the dead need help in adjusting to their new situation. Therefore, if there was any chance that John's spirit was getting some tiny and inexplicable benefit out of my taking homeopathic preparations, then the experience was unquestionably worthwhile.

16

BIRTHDAY GIFT

All of this – the chaos of difficult emotions, the extreme responses, the self-analysis, the mystical events – were exhausting. I needed a break from it and my birthday was approaching. Rather than dread it, I decided to do something about it. Glenda, an old friend, was staying in Northern Thailand for a few months and had invited me to visit. John had left a sizeable number of frequent-flyer points in his airline account and, although I had informed the airline that he was dead, the account had not been deleted. Using his points to fly to Thailand in luxurious business class would be a terrific way to mark my birthday but I was not optimistic that I would be permitted to use the account. Nevertheless I rang the airline with my fingers crossed.

'Oh, look at this,' exclaimed the cheerful man at the other end of the phone. 'There is no first class on this flight so I can get you the best seat in the plane.' Without discussion or argument, I got a return flight to Bangkok courtesy of John. His magical manipulation had struck again.

Glenda and I were driven out of Chiang Mai by a young Thai man who had no English but was a trusted contact of Glenda's. 'My Thai friends have told him that we want to see wats and we would like some surprises,' she explained by way of an itinerary.

For four days our driver brought us to temples of every description: small ones, large ones, busy ones, isolated ones, temples on the tourist map and temples in obscure places. On my birthday he drove us through Chiang Rai and out to a river where he stopped the car. Smiling, he gestured at us to go to a hut by the brown water. There were several long boats tied to the bank by the shed.

'Trust,' said Glenda encouragingly. 'We said we wanted surprises so let's go.'

There were a couple of men in the hut behind a table. We worked out they were selling a boat trip – to where or for how long, we had no idea. We handed over some money and set off. Farms lined the river. Occasionally there was a house but mostly it was green farmland with people working in the fields. The silent boatman pulled into the bank and pointed to the side of a 200-ft rock outcrop.

'Well' said Glenda, surveying the scene. There was a forest beside the outcrop. The air was silent. 'Come on, we're here, somewhere, we're not going to turn back now.'

We followed the track around the side of the outcrop and saw stone steps cut into the side of it. It led to a massive cave with several enormous Buddha statues set into natural grottos. Bats clung to the roof of each grotto. There was lino on the floor. The place was silent. A tangible energy wrapped itself around us, allowing us to float in our bare feet through this magical place. When we had our fill of the energy, we floated back to our boatman beaming happily like a pair of old hippies. The boat roared off, heading further down the river. We were marvelling at the secret place we had been taken to and how good it was to know local people when three long boats came around the bend of the river. They were full of what sounded like German tourists; there must have been about eighty of them and most were armed with video recorders. It turned out that they were heading for a highlight of the Chiang Rai tourist trail: the grotto in the rock outcrop.

Our boat pulled into a village where our driver was waiting with our air-conditioned car. Two elephants were tethered near the water while several others were working. Stalls selling souvenirs lined the road up from the river. I wanted to get myself a birthday present and browsed the stalls. Then, through the clatter of a busy market, I was drawn to the sound of a gong. I turned around: a stall-holder I had passed was looking at me, calling me back. I couldn't resist and the gong became my present.

My birthday, the first after John's death and the anniversary of the vodka incident, had been a joy.

17

FIRST ANNIVERSARY

'Mark all anniversaries carefully,' Mary had advised on several occasions. My birthday had certainly proved the value of this advice. There had been no heartache and the magical moment in the Buddha grotto had been a bonus I would remember forever. Now the first anniversary of John's death was approaching. I had been alone in New Guinea for the first anniversary of Mike's death and had handled it badly. It had occurred six weeks after I arrived and I had told only one colleague about Mike's death. I asked this colleague if she would be free to do something, anything, that day.

'No,' she said, 'I'm busy.' Then for some strange reason she added, 'You know, Cath, you made the decision to leave Ireland. You are on your own and it's times like these when it will be difficult, but it was your choice to be by yourself, never forget that.'

As a seasoned expat who had spent about fifteen years travelling from continent to continent and university to university, my colleague knew what she was talking about. Of course it had been my choice to leave Ireland so soon after Mike's death but now I had no idea what to do; I had never had to commemorate such an event before. On the evening of the anniversary, I sat on the veranda of my flat smoking cigarettes and looking blankly down the hill and over the trees surrounding the university houses and apartments. The air was dead quiet. There was no busyness, no sound of cars, no people, no children playing and no background noise; the silence was broken only by the occasional outburst of a cicada. The momentous nature of what the day stood for had hung like a weight over me and I had no idea what to do with it. Eventually, mercifully, the day ended and it was time to go to bed.

Despite the quietness and my complete ignorance about grief, I knew even then that there had been something at best unhelpful and at worst deeply destructive about the way I had spent the first anniversary of Mike's death. I was not going to get caught like that on John's first anniversary. Mass, the great Irish tradition, was out of the question. The only Catholic ceremonies I had been to in Melbourne had been weddings. I did not know any priests or churches and did not want to approach a priest for fear of giving the impression that I might be interested in attending a church regularly – a hangover from childhood, I suppose. During the year Robert, Samantha and myself had scattered John's ashes in the sea. Some old friends with a yacht moored in the bay had taken us out to sea for the simple ceremony. It now made sense to involve the sea in an anniversary ceremony but how and where, I couldn't decide.

Then a series of coincidences occurred. Firstly I picked the rune stone, *Jera*, more frequently than before. *Jera* is also known as *One Year* and refers to patience and perseverance:

Be mindful that patience is essential for the recognition of your own process, which, in its season, leads to the harvest of the self.

I had picked it a few times in the previous six months but now it was appearing nearly every second evening. It wasn't so much the interpretation as the title, 'one year' that struck me forcibly. There was no doubt in my mind that John was saying hello. It was a very comforting thought to take to bed.

Two relevant pieces of music were broadcast on the radio while I was pondering what to do. It was odd to hear the song, 'Red Roses for a Blue Lady', several times during those weeks. John and I had danced to it at a party in our house the last winter he had been alive. John had loved dancing. He had also been a romantic: at least once a year he had sent me an enormous bunch of flowers at work, sometimes for my birthday or our anniversary and sometimes for no reason at all. Hearing this song gave me an idea: 'I'll get a dozen red roses and put one into the sea,' I thought. Another element of the ceremony was now in place.

The other song was Van Morrison's love song, 'Have I Told You Lately that I Love You'. It is a popular song but it seemed to be on the radio an inordinate number of times prior to John's anniversary. During the six months before he died, John had gone to the trouble of finding that song on a CD and playing it to me several times – loudly. Each time was a surprise because he had never done anything like that before. Now here it was, being broadcast nearly every time I turned on the radio. 'Good one, John. Thank you.' I was happy to believe that he had knowingly set that song up as a message before he killed himself. Each time I heard it, it inevitably produced tears, but the tears were of the sad, melancholy variety rather than the ferocious wails of distraught emotion.

Warren and Garry invited me to lunch in the country near the sea and so the day took shape: flowers, a late lunch and then I would go to the beach.

As I was getting ready to leave my apartment, the midday movie was on television in the background. It was a film based on a Danielle Steel book where a young woman is left widowed when her older husband dies; of course, I noted with mild frustration, it happens early enough in the film so the heroine can fall in love again before the film ends. Accompanied by the usual poignant music, the heroine browses through a gift she received from her late husband, *Sonnets from the Portuguese*, a book of love sonnets by Elizabeth Barrett Browning. That caught my attention. John had also given me a present of an expensive edition of *Sonnets from the Portuguese* and often quoted the famous lines, 'How do I love thee? Let me count the ways.' That was as far as he ever got and, not being overly fond of poetry, I had never read the whole sonnet. Without thinking, I grabbed the cloth-bound edition on my way out the door; reading a piece of poetry while throwing a flower into the water seemed suitably melodramatic for an anniversary ceremony.

*

Later that day, as the warm sun moved towards the horizon, I walked along the empty beach to the water's edge and threw a rose into the waves of Bass Strait. The sea kept washing the rose back to the shore, it had no intention of drifting away romantically. As it rolled on the sand with the waves, I read the sonnet to the sun as part of the ceremony. The last lines were astounding:

> . . . *I love thee with the breath,*
> *Smiles, tears, of all of my life! – and, if God choose,*
> *I shall but love thee better after death.*

Had John known that these were the last lines of the sonnet? Had he even read them? 'How do I love thee, let me count the ways' – that was the only line of this sonnet he ever uttered. This was way beyond the bounds of coincidence. Had he known this was how it ended and simply left it there waiting for me until now? There was no flippancy in my wonder any more.

I sat in the car in the evening sun listening to Van Morrison until the time went past 6.50 p.m., the moment to the year that John had shot himself, then drove back to Melbourne. John's first anniversary had passed without ugly heartache. In fact the day had more than just passed: the odd collection of ceremonies had turned the day into one of melancholy gentleness.

18

NEW YEAR'S EVE

Moments when I felt peaceful and completely relaxed were rare as I moved into the second year of grief. Part of me was definitely in another world, somewhere out in the universe with John and that was the part of me that knew peace when it was left alone. Had I been able to stay on the veranda of the farm or sit in the desert indefinitely looking at the trees and the birds, I might have been calm forever.

But the detail involved in living on earth barged in time and again to shatter the peace. Administrative matters, work, trying to stay socially connected – everything that involved living in the real world caused pain and discomfort. Nothing came easily or naturally. My body was in constant and mostly inexplicable pain. It was a year after John's death and I was an emotional basket case, crying at nothing and fearful of talking to people. My head maintained a running conversation about anything and everything, keeping me awake at night and adding to the struggle of the day. I had no doubt but that it was all the standard stuff of grief but in a flash I had gone from being a competent, professional woman with a beloved husband, a good social life and plenty of interests and activities, to being a reclusive widow who would see no one for days and preferring it that way.

'This is the work,' I reminded myself. 'This is grief, you accepted it.'

Somewhere beyond my normal consciousness, I could sense a voice was encouraging me, assuring me that I could do this and that it was, in fact, a good and worthy thing to do. The voice was accompanied by a brief sensation of strength and even, weirdly, excitement. In moments like this, I urged myself along by humming 'You'll Never Walk Alone', or by calling on images of climbing mountains, travelling though unmarked tracks in the desert or struggling through muck, all of which helped to keep me going.

'As long as I don't stop,' I said repeatedly, 'I won't go under.'

At one particularly critical moment, I was helped along by a prayer from a small, pocket prayer book that someone had given me and which I had shoved into my handbag. I wasn't having much luck with traditional prayers, the language or the sentiments irritated me more often than not; childhood again, I supposed. Then, for want of something to read on a tram, I found this prayer by Francis de Sales:

> *The everlasting God has in His wisdom foreseen from eternity the cross that He now presents to you as a gift from His inmost heart. This cross He now sends you He has considered with His all-knowing eyes, understood with His divine mind, tested with His wise justice, warmed with His loving arms, and weighted with His own hands to see that*

it be not one inch too large and not one ounce too heavy for you. He has blessed it with His holy name, anointed it with His grace, perfumed it with His consolation, taken one last glance at you and your courage, and then sent it to you from heaven, a special greeting from God to you, an alms of the all-merciful love of God.

It was as powerful a message as any I received during this time and for some inexplicable reason, given my ambivalence to old-fashioned prayers, I found it very reassuring. 'What doesn't kill you makes you stronger,' it said to me, 'and you're well able for this. It's tough but you're strong and capable of taking this on.' The delicate, inner voice agreed.

*

Very occasionally, despite my careful management, the grief erupted uncontrollably in public situations and on New Year's Eve, just over a year after John had died, it came to a head when I made an error of judgement. Instead of planning the day as I had done my birthday, John's anniversary and Christmas, I choose New Year's Eve to go to a bank and transfer the bulk of my money from a complicated savings account to a cheque account. I wanted to send it to an investment broker early in the new year. It was a Monday and very hot, the local shopping area was jam-packed, two men bulging out of a small red sports car stole my car parking spot and I was frazzled by the time I got to the bank. It was air-conditioned and hushed as banks usually are. The queue was long but it was a pleasant enough space. I relaxed. My turn came. I handed over the various bits of paper to swap the money from one account to the other.

'This is a joint account, I will need Mr Johnson's signature to transfer this much money,' the teller said.

I was jolted out of automatic pilot.

'No!' I nearly yelled at her. 'No,' I said more quietly. *Stay calm, it's not her fault.* My head was now working overtime. 'My husband is dead and I have sent several copies of his death cert and will to the bank,' I explained, launching into a very brief history of my relationship with the bank over the previous year. 'Now I just want to transfer the money to the cheque account and leave.'

'I'm sorry, I can't transfer it without seeing an authorised death certificate and a will,' the teller was sympathetic but subject to procedure.

I stared at her in disbelief. How could anyone in this bank be unaware that my husband, John, had died dramatically in December 2000? Short of going to the bank's Christmas party and announcing it, it felt like I had told just about everyone who worked in this organisation that he was no longer with us. But somehow there was no record of my frequent communications with the bank attached to this particular account.

Fighting tears, I insisted that the bank had made an error in its administration. The queue ran parallel to the tellers; there were another six tellers in operation so I was not delaying anyone but the queue was close enough for people to tune into the story if they wanted to; once again I suspected I was entertaining bored people with my drama. I tried to keep my voice low but could feel hysterics threatening. The teller did her best, ringing various people to find out if indeed a death cert for John had been lodged anywhere else in the bank.

An hour later the transaction was completed but I was a total mess. For the first time I had broken down in a public place. Over the year the bank had certainly given me plenty of opportunity to release anger but I thought we had reached a point of mutual cooperation. Clearly we had not, although my extreme response probably had less to do with frustration with the bank than with how I was really feeling. I had managed the emotive day badly; some basic planning would have made this situation easy to avoid. It was too early after John died to take any emotive day for granted so, however frustrating it might be, it was still clearly necessary to put time and effort into avoiding distressing situations.

19

SELF-ABSORPTION

Brenda left Melbourne in March 2002. I had been with her for nearly eighteen months, seeing her for an hour on average two weeks out of every three. I was very sorry to see her go but also interested in whether I could stand on my own feet for a while. She recommended another counsellor whom I agreed to see. In the meantime I had bought a round-the-world business class ticket and was going to Brazil, Ireland and Paris over a four-week period.

The one dread prior to this trip was whether I could handle the sight of happy tourist couples because, irrationally, I was beginning to feel a bit jealous of couples. Fortunately British Airways business class was luxurious and set up for people by themselves and my friends in Brazil were independent people who were having a relaxed break in a fishing village near Florianopolis. There was an opportunity to stay in Rio for a couple of days but I was nervous about it: holiday hotels are usually full of couples.

'Why are you staying in a budget hotel?' Warren asked browsing through a brochure of hotels in Rio. 'Look at this one; Princess Diana stayed here. This is definitely the place for you.'

'The Copacabaña Palace Hotel. Are you mad? Did you see the price for one night?'

'You can afford it. You're working, you have the pensions, that's what they're for. Do you want to stay in a cheap hotel surrounded by families or do you want to be a glamorous, single woman travelling the world? You can sit by the pool looking elegant and drinking margaritas.'

The very idea of staying in a family tourist hotel was intimidating, even for one night. And whatever about me being elegant or glamorous – it had been a struggle to maintain any interest in my appearance since John died – the Copacabaña Palace Hotel was much more appealing and potentially far less stressful. I agreed to spend my money on luxury.

'Great,' Warren smiled. 'I'll be waiting to hear about it and bring me back a soap.'

A sense of adventure flickered around the edges of my visit to Brazil. I had never been to South America before and I did not know the people I was meeting up with very well. The prospect of new experiences made me feel alive again.

*

Warren had been inspired. Staying at the beautiful hotel in Rio was absolutely the right thing to do. There was no intrusive sense of families and couples. The atmosphere was so comfortable that I even went on a tour in a small group where I teamed up with an older English widow who was spending her time travelling. Couples holding each other's knees on the train up to Corcovado did not upset me at all.

I had a cocktail by the hotel pool and packed a soap for Warren.

I had felt a similar degree of excitement in Singapore when I had stopped over there on the way to New Guinea in 1985. Now, however, there was an added element. In 1985 I had had no experience of visiting exotic cities but it had not made me nervous because I had nothing to lose. In 2002 I was a more seasoned traveller but was carrying a greater sense of loss. The challenge was now to be in the world without that massive sense of loss and perhaps – eventually, hopefully – a renewed sense of excitement.

*

Being surrounded by people again in Ireland was challenging. I was by now far more aware of the contrast between my life and the lives of everyone around me. My family and friends seemed engaged in the ordinary flow of their lives, looking after their children, managing responsibilities, confronting problems and generally living in the real world. Even my father, then aged 84 and slowing down, was more alive than I was, pursuing his research on the River Liffey, preparing a lecture and finding energy for lengthy conversations over a bottomless pot of tea. Grief had clearly made mincemeat of me and I was desperate for peace of mind, to be normal again, but could not remember what that meant any more.

Was my self-absorption due entirely to John's death or had I lost the plot somewhere along the way? Was my isolation feeding the intensity of the grief or was I in fact privileged in having the space to allow the grief to run its natural course without interruption? That I had no responsibilities was unquestionably a feature of this whole process. John's two children were living in Adelaide with his ex-wife when we met. Samantha had lived with us for several years when she was a teenager; she was now an adult with a child of her own. Robert remained in Adelaide and was also an adult when John died. There was no role other than friendship for me there.

During my holiday in Dublin in 2002, I went to Paris with two nieces. As the aunt responsible for a nine-year old and a seventeen-year old, there was no time for neurosis and self-absorption. In the lift going to the top of the Eiffel Tower, I tried to protect my youngest niece from the shrill voice of an American woman who was winding up her twelve-year old boy into a state of paralysis by pointing out loudly that the spike was dangerously narrow. In EuroDisney the test was to try and source reasonable food when several restaurants were closed and the queues at the other outlets were lengthy. It was also to ensure the young people's well-being on the wild Space Mountain ride; in the exhilaration of the ride, I could only hope that safety regulations were as strictly enforced in France as they were in Australia. By the end of four days, I had forgotten myself.

'Maybe that's how other people get through grief without all the drama I seem to be creating,' I thought about it on the way back to Melbourne. 'People with responsibilities in their lives simply don't have the space to be so self-absorbed because other people are relying on them.'

But the thought was exhausting: how did people who had children and responsibilities get through their grief? I might have been self-absorbed but I certainly wasn't putting on the pain and exhaustion. I did not know whether I was lucky or unlucky to have no one to look after, but that was the way it was.

*

John and I had never intended to have children of our own but it had led to a situation that inadvertently gave me the first clue that John could be very decisive and that he had a destructive way of dealing with problems in his life. At the end of 1986, not long before he was due to complete his tour of duty in Papua New Guinea, we were having brunch on the veranda of his house surrounded by tropical plants and tropical sounds.

'Are you sure you don't want any children?' asked John suddenly.

'Yes, sure, positive, no question about it.' We had talked about the issue briefly in the early days of our relationship and the topic had never come up again.

'If you want kids, I'd be happy to have more children,' he said.

'No, love, I don't. Why do you ask?'

'You might change your mind in your thirties.'

'Yeah,' I laughed, 'I've heard that before. But seriously, no, I actually feel lucky that I know for definite that I don't want children.'

Several girlfriends in Moresby had spoken with angst about the prospect of ending up in their forties, childless. One had been trying for years with her husband and was in Papua New Guinea now as a compensation for their lack of success. Another was ambivalent but her husband was not – he did not want kids, or so he told us all at a dinner party one evening when they had thrown their personal discussion on the subject open to the table. Several other women either did not have a male partner at all or a partner with whom they wanted to have children. Listening to these conversations, I was able to work through my own attitude to having children and realised that there was nothing in me that wanted a child.

'If you're sure,' said John.

'I'm sure.'

'Well then I'm going to get the unkindest snip of all,' the serious, determined look was replaced by a broad grin. 'I've booked in for Thursday.'

'What? A vasectomy? Isn't that a drastic step? Would you not wait until you are in Australia?'

'All I needed to do was to be sure you didn't want kids. No more messing about and no more uncertainty. Joe's snip and tuck worked very well, I'll get the same man to do it, can't go wrong.'

Joe was a friend who had had a successful and painless vasectomy in a local clinic a few weeks beforehand. While it suited me very well that John would have a vasectomy, I could not help noticing that he had just made an enormous decision about his life with only a word to me at the last minute. I have no doubt but that he would have held off if I had wanted children but he clearly had no intention of throwing his decision open to discussion. Nevertheless I liked his decisiveness: it demonstrated a strength of character I admired in him.

John had a vasectomy under local anaesthetic and he watched the whole procedure with fascination. He treated the procedure as if he had just had a tooth extraction. A few days later he developed an infection. He was barely able to walk and could only wear a sarong although it did not stop him going out to any of the end-of-year parties. Despite his good humour, he was in constant and excruciating pain. As an army officer in a difficult posting, he had an emergency medical kit that included heavy-duty painkillers and sleeping pills; he worked his way through those. He also drank alcohol to distract himself from the pain. I tried to persuade him to ease off on the cocktail.

'The pain is too terrible, I have to do something,' he would moan, looking miserable as he laid there, whisky bottle to hand.

When he ran out of medication, he called the doctor. Lying on the sofa with the bottle of whisky, John related his sorry tale, emphasising the degree of pain he was suffering. The young male doctor, squirming in his chair, empathised far too much.

'Mate, what can I say? Take whatever helps you with the pain,' he advised, writing out another prescription.

'Are you sure it is safe to drink alcohol and take all of those pills?' I interrupted.

John and the doctor exchanged knowing glances.

'Look mate, you take what you need to take. The infection is under control and the swelling will go down, it shouldn't be long now. But in the meantime do whatever you need to do to get through it.'

Damn! John was pumping a cocktail of alcohol and pills into his system and all the doctor could do was encourage him. One Friday afternoon, four weeks after the operation, John rang me at work. He was slurring his words and I could barely understand him.

'Get home if you can,' was the message I deciphered. He was in trouble.

I rang a friend and asked her to keep talking to John until I got home. My fear – based on total ignorance – was that John would slip into a coma. When I got there, he was on the floor, muttering into the phone. For an hour or two, he drifted in and out of conversation, sometimes being cheeky to me, sometimes being worried about his own condition. Then two friends arrived; fortunately word had travelled through our network of friends.

'John, you silly bugger, what have you taken?' asked

Mike, walking into the house.

'Leave the boys to it,' Glenda said to me. 'We'll go out for coffee.'

Several hours later we returned and Mike and John were roaring their heads off in laughter.

'I have just been getting a lecture about becoming a strung-out junkie,' said John, looking much better. 'This old bugger has told me to stop self-medicating.'

'You're so pious about illegal drugs but you're doing exactly the same thing with the legal stuff,' said Mike. I never found out what Mike had said when they had been alone but whatever it was, it worked. John gave up the cocktail and quickly returned to his more usual healthy, cheerful state.

I had no idea then that John's kamikaze behaviour and decisiveness would be replayed much later on in our relationship, ending in his death. If I had had a crystal ball, it still would not have stopped me marrying him. But perhaps, if I had been more aware of these things, I might have been able to find a way to help him long before his post-traumatic stress overwhelmed him.

20

WAITING FOR GRIEF TO PASS

Back in Melbourne after the round-the-world trip, it was again difficult to know quite what I was doing there. I could chat to John in spirit but that was not location-specific – although whether I could have sustained it to the same degree surrounded by loving people was questionable. Work was functional but not particularly pleasurable. Warren and close friends were essential but geography did not limit the degree of friendship with them. Brenda had left and so had my yoga teacher. The only significant property I owned in Australia was the large car. All that kept me in the country was the decision I had made when John died that I would make no major decision until the two-year grieving period was up. I had another eight months to go and I was determined to adhere to the plan. Anyway, Melbourne had been good to me since 1987 and all the practicalities of my life were there, providing continuity and routine.

*

In 1987 the Australian Army had posted John to Melbourne after the completion of his tour of duty in Papua New Guinea, which is why we ended up there. Initially I worked part-time to give me an opportunity to become used to my new surroundings. John was in his new army posting – which he was not happy with. Two months after we arrived, he rang me at work.

'I've quit the army,' he announced. 'They've given me the very posting I specifically said I didn't want. So that's it. After twenty-three years I'm out. I'll be on the standard three months' notice.'

John had joined the army in 1964, a year after leaving England. When he had first arrived in Australia, the Big Brother Movement had put him on a farm in rural New South Wales. It was extremely hard work and the conditions were harsh. He slept in a barn, was up long before dawn and had to wash in water from a cold tap before milking the cows. Then he rode to the farmhouse for breakfast where the farmer's wife poured pure cream onto his breakfast cereal.

'She said I was too scrawny for farm work and had to be fattened up,' he remembered. 'She was right, I was much smaller than I am now. And how I loved that pure cream!'

He worked six long days a week and had to go to church on Sunday morning, which left him with only Sunday afternoon to himself. The pay was minimal and he was in the middle of nowhere, so there was nothing to do except hang out with the other farmhand.

He learnt a lot in the brief period he was there, including how to handle cows and horses, make fences and drive a farm utility. Once when he washed in a dam, the farmer beat him severely for contaminating the animals' drinking water – the city boy had to learn fast. Despite the hardship, he remembered the farmer and his wife fondly. After a month, however, he had had enough and used his pay to return to Sydney. Although angry with him for leaving his job, the Big Brother official found him another job, this time in a department store. Shortly afterwards he quit that and joined the army. The structure, security and fraternity of the army suited him very well. Starting as a private at the age of seventeen, he went steadily through the ranks, was commissioned as an officer and finished with the rank of major.

John's decision to leave the army in 1987 was sudden and a surprise; I had no idea that it was coming. After two months' unemployment – and refusing jobs that did not offer him enough money for what they were asking him to do – he secured employment on a major logistical project with a large accountancy firm. He remained with that firm working on major projects until he died. His period of unemployment was a nerve-wracking time. As an emigrant from 1980s Ireland, I presumed that jobs were scarce and any opportunity should be grabbed regardless of quality. John was not having any of that and preferred to head off into Victoria's gold fields with a metal detector rather than grab the first job that was offered to him.

With minimal savings I had to abandon my pleasant part-time job and look for a full-time library position. It was a culture shock to find that I had the pick of four different jobs. None was startling, nor was any a promotion on my position in New Guinea but as a new arrival to Australia I did not expect that. I chose one that was not especially dynamic or challenging but would allow me to find my feet in Melbourne without undue stress.

For diversion and as a way of settling into an alien community, I undertook a Master of Arts by thesis on the history of Melbourne Zoo. Over the next few years, this project took off and I became the Zoo's honorary historian. It involved giving lectures, writing publications and generally becoming knowledgeable about the history and development of one of the city's major institutions. It was a very enjoyable way of getting to know the city and its culture. I also went from totally disapproving the concept of zoos to understanding the role a good, modern zoo can play in contemporary society.

I maintained my contact with Melbourne Zoo after John died. Five days after John's funeral in December 2000, my sisters had peeled me off the veranda to deliver a presentation I had already agreed to give to the management of the Zoo. I rehearsed the talk thoroughly, Anna produced Powerpoint slides as my prompters and I delivered it, confident that no one listening would know what had happened during the previous fortnight. It was only when participants came up to talk to me afterwards that I realised I was incapable of doing anything other than delivering the prepared talk and left quickly.

Thereafter I continued to deliver my usual talks at the Zoo. The Zoo friends and staff were always warm and welcoming so it was an easy environment to be in, even when I was feeling perturbed. But there was no question of pursuing Melbourne Zoo's history any further; that part of my life was over.

21

LETTING JOHN GO

By September 2002 my apparent lack of progress through the quagmire of grief was beginning to concern me. John was dead twenty months by now and my routine was fairly steady, yet I was constantly agitated and self-conscious and there seemed little hope that I would feel normal again by December, which was when my allocated two years of grieving would be over. If anything I felt I was getting worse and could unravel any minute. This feeling started when I began to think that John's spirit was about to leave my orbit. It was a thought that originated so quietly I had not noticed it when it came to me first; but gradually the thought became louder and more insistent.

'I can't do it to you any longer, can I?' I addressed John's spirit, which I imagined was floating above me. 'I'm dragging you back into a place where you don't want to be now by constantly talking to you and asking for help.'

I waited for the emptiness to protest and say it was OK to continue to draw John's spirit into my earthly routine.

Nothing happened, no sense of anything supportive came to me.

'I have to let you go, don't I?' I announced reluctantly.

Again no protest. By now I had learnt to read my physical reactions to big questions and in this instance my body was agreeing it was time to let John go. There had been nothing rational about my relationship with John in spirit and there was nothing rational about this realisation. But in the context in which I had talked to him for well over a year now, I knew it was time.

*

I had let him go before – when he had been alive. Such was his condition in the last eighteen months of his life that three times I had told him he did not need to stay around for me – and each time I meant that he did not have to stay alive for me. The first time was when he was so distraught that I believed he was very ill and probably dying. Everything he said and did, awake or asleep, suggested that living was a massive struggle and that he did not want to continue. After a tense and emotional fortnight, I eventually accepted that I could not hold onto him if he wanted to die. One night, when he was sobbing deeply in his sleep, I whispered to him he did not need to stay alive for me.

The second time I had told him he did not have to go on living for my sake was when he was in one of his tormented, half-asleep, half-awake states; again he had been sobbing deeply, holding my hand hard into his chest, talking with anguish about something almost indecipherable and saying he didn't want to go on living. I again said quietly that he did not have to stay alive for my sake. I have no idea whether he registered what I was saying on a conscious level.

The third time he had seemed to be awake but in a very deep and dark place and talking about killing himself. His eyes were focussed on something far away; when he did look at me in response to my voice, he seemed puzzled, as if he was trying to work out who I was. That happened not long before he died. He had been so sad, so very deeply and hopelessly sad, I again said that he didn't have to put himself through the torture of living just so that I would not be alone. Although he seemed conscious, I don't know if he heard me. He seldom remembered conversations that occurred when he was in that state but I felt he needed to hear me give him permission to leave if that was what he wanted to do.

Now, twenty months after he died, I had to let him go yet again. *Let the winds of heaven dance between you . . .* the *Partnership* rune came out of the bag a few times to encourage me. I went for a walk on the beach in the dark. The moon was nearly full and was high in the sky. This was the moment I felt with great certainty that John was saying goodbye and heading off. I looked up. A second moon appeared. I squinted and rearranged my eyes. There were still two moons and nothing else had doubled. The second moon remained for minutes then vanished as I was watching. He was gone.

22

DISCARDING THE WIDOW'S BLACK

With no crutch, no one to hold onto in spirit or otherwise, I was more jittery than ever. 'You should get massage,' a woman said one day. 'My husband was away for six weeks and getting a massage was all I could do to keep myself sane, I missed him so much.'

That comment hurt a lot.

'The answers are in yourself, you don't need another person to fulfil you,' another married acquaintance told me when I foolishly allowed her to tap into the emotional difficulties of life without my husband. 'People of your age often prefer their own company anyway, it is not unusual.'

That comment also got me where it hurt and I fled back to my apartment to hide. My reaction surprised me. For the first time since John died, casual comments made by acquaintances were now getting to me. For eighteen months virtually nothing anyone had said upset me. Expressions like 'I need that like a hole in the head,' or 'biting the bullet' did not bother me. Questions about my guilt level or any concern I might have about the stigma of suicide were peculiar but did not stress me either. Now, however, a reference to someone's misery when her husband was away for six weeks, the sight of loving couples in restaurants or tourist couples trying to read a map in the wind had the power to stir me up. Was it because I was coming out of the daze and realising how much I was missing John? Or perhaps it was the prospect of being alone forever that was so terrifying. My only method for dealing with this was to try and ignore it and not give into self-pity or tears.

*

A confrontation with an ill-mannered man had the most remarkable and practical impact on the progress of my grief. It had happened one day when the new acquaintance was exceptionally rude to me while being charming to everyone else in the group I was with at the time. I had never met the man before and I knew the cause of his rudeness was political rather than personal. However it was a very unsettling encounter. I walked home severely rattled, blood pounding through the veins in my head, boxing matches flaring under my skin and my mind working overtime to try and explain this out of my system.

'Stop this, stop this,' I told myself. 'The man is a dickhead . . .' (sometimes coarse language was irresistible), 'but it's not personal. There is nothing at all personal in his attack.'

I walked on. 'Find a reason for thanking him for this,' I thought repeatedly.

In 1999, I had read Carolyn Myss's book, *Anatomy of the Spirit*. I liked the practical approach to life that she presented in her writing. In one instance, she talked about her response to a challenge by a gruff person at one of her seminars. 'I'm going to sit here next to you until I can think of a reason to thank you for that comment,' she said to the woman. 'We might be here for a very long time.' After a period of tension, Carolyn Myss found a reason that radically changed her approach to her work. She thanked the woman: 'I think you just might have saved my life. I am grateful to you,' she said. I had used the concept several times after reading it but had not used it much since John died. Now it was time to revitalise it.

'Find a reason to thank him,' I walked on under the large, old trees of St Kilda Road muttering crossly. 'Find a reason. Find a reason.'

Suddenly it clicked. I was so shocked I stood still for a second with my mouth open. Fortunately there were few other walkers; it was winter.

'That man didn't treat me like a widow; he didn't give a damn what my state of mind was. He's on his own mission and couldn't care less whether I'm fragile or not.'

After John had died, an email was sent to over 300 library staff and a collection was organised for the Vietnam Veterans Association. At first it was a bit disconcerting that everyone knew John had died dramatically but at least I could presume that everyone was aware of my state of mind. Whether that influenced the way my colleagues worked with me, I had no idea, I was beyond noticing. This man was the first person who had been outright rude to me since John died – at least the first person I had noticed being rude.

'Why should he treat me like a widow?' I reasoned. 'Why should anyone treat me like a widow? Have I been manipulating my status of widowhood to get out of living in the real world?'

Of course I had – I had to in order to survive. For a while I needed to be a widow, to wrap the black cloak of widowhood around me and respond to demands on my time or energy by saying – silently – 'no, sorry, I am a grieving widow, go away.'

Now it was time to stop that; it was time to throw off the widow's black cloak and don the widow's purple. Somewhere in childhood I had learnt of the tradition that a widow wore black for the first year of bereavement and purple for the second. This suited me: I wasn't ready to be a complete non-widow because that would suggest that my grieving process was over and I was single again; I was a long way from being able to handle that concept. However I was ready to move into the next stage of widowhood, into the traditional purple phase. The shift felt almost physical. Being a widow was no longer a full-time part of my identity.

'Thank you,' I thought sincerely to the man who had been rude to me. 'I still don't much like your style but I will thank you forever for what you have just given me.'

23

POST-TRAUMATIC STRESS UNLEASHED

After the first euphoric flush at being finished with deep widowhood, my condition became more severe than ever. By removing the widow's black cloak, I seemed to have also removed a layer of protection because the cocoon effect of being in a total daze had vanished. I felt more raw and horrible then ever and the pain was relentless. Even the threat of being reincarnated to complete all of this grief on a rubbish dump in the Philippines was losing its motivational power.

The feeling of impending meltdown became more intense during October 2002. My head was rattling, my body was sore and jumpy, I couldn't sleep at all without the help of a Valium, there was a lot of anger in my dreams, I cried easily, and was constantly depressed and miserable. Most worrying of all, I had even lost the ability to see my grief objectively. The little voice in the back of my head that had been urging me on had vanished, the pain was becoming intolerable and I was losing interest in caring what happened to me. My new counsellor lived on the other side of the city and I saw her every six weeks or so.

'Stop this,' I nagged. 'It is now nearly two years, your serious grieving time is up in December.'

It didn't feel like two years, it felt like yesterday. Techniques Brenda had taught me to find a moment's peace were not working any more; I simply could not create a calm enough space to use them properly and I was becoming frantic. Work and my routine continued as usual but it was tough holding them together. In November I was on the brink of a meltdown. Warren was watching.

'Take a couple of weeks off; you have the sick leave, use it. Whatever is happening at the moment, it looks rough from this perspective.'

My work manager, Kerrie, was also watching. She had been one of my key supporters over the two years. When my work was flagging, she pushed gently to maintain my standards; when I was spaced out, she took me out to coffee in one of the nearby cafes to discuss work and whatever else came up. Her curiosity with the process and chaos of grief was similar to Warren's. She was interested in the practical side of it, allowing me to discuss and tease through whatever drama I had surrounded myself with. It led to insights on my part but was never therapy. Our conversations had more to do with the unfolding story of grief then with resolving emotional and other issues. Now Kerrie was concerned about me.

'Something has happened, you don't seem too well,' she said sympathetically while looking enquiringly at me.

I nearly burst out crying on the spot. Somehow Kerrie's words of concern had managed to get through whatever defences I had erected to ensure self-control in public.

'I don't know why but these last weeks have been pretty awful. It's as if something has happened. After Mike, I knew that the second year would be worse than the first because I would notice more. Maybe that happened when I shifted from widow's black to widow's purple.' Kerrie was familiar with that story.

She agreed that I should take a couple of weeks off to sort myself out. Although we were similar ages and good friends, her response was almost motherly. In fact she was one of the few mothers in my close Australian circle of friends and perhaps there was something in her tone that penetrated my defences this time. I went home and collapsed, exhausted physically, mentally and emotionally.

*

Over the next fortnight I had nights of upsetting dreams, which usually involved images of John, distressed and angry, with a damaged head and pain in his eyes. In the dreams I tried helplessly to fix things, to help him manage his troubles, to heal him. When I was awake I tried to see John, to conjure up his face, to relive the fun and happiness we had shared for so long but I couldn't get anything at all. All I could remember when I thought about him as a human were the troubles of the last year and a half of his life, the extreme events of his last month and his final days. By talking to John in spirit and establishing a spirit relationship with him since he died, I had ignored thinking about his troubles on earth. Creating a sense of him in spirit had been much easier than trying to imagine a happy, living John.

But it was clear I could no longer avoid confronting those last months when John's post-traumatic stress began to dominate our lives. The confrontation had to be honest, human and real – the horrors as well as the fun, the trauma and frustration as well as the excitement. There was no space for spiritual escapism or delusions here; my dreams and the pains in my body were becoming more ferocious by the day so it was now time to face all of that. Something prompted me to open my computer and write. This quickly turned into an uncontrolled deluge of memory of the build-up to his suicide.

*

The medical problems had started appearing in 1995 when his heart was diagnosed as having an arrhythmia. He was forty-seven by then, the same age as his father had been when he had died. This seemed to play on John's mind because he mentioned it numerous times. Over the next three years stress-related illnesses insidiously began to affect all parts of his body. He had problems with his heart, cholesterol and blood pressure, and he developed diabetes. He was also having bad night sweats, which the doctors did not relate directly to his diabetes.

'My body's rejecting me,' was his usual comment when he had to add another pill to his daily intake.

Each Anzac Day, 25 April, he joined his mates from the unit he had served with in Vietnam. The commemoration involves a parade of war veterans interspersed with marching bands. The veterans wear their medals and a sprig of rosemary attached to a tiny Australian flag for remembrance, which is given to them at the march. Each year John kept the rosemary and flag with his medals in a wooden box that he had made himself.

'The year I don't get rosemary on Anzac Day is the year I'll die,' he said each year as he prepared himself for the march.

I knew it was a very important day for him; it was the only time in the year where he could talk about – or at least refer to – his experiences in Vietnam. He seldom spoke about his tour of duty in Vietnam and when he did, the stories related to non-combat events. Once, when I was visiting my sister alone in Saigon, I rang him from the banks of the Saigon River to say hello.

'I used to go fishing there,' he sounded excited. 'I spotted an old guy fishing in the river and went to see what he was catching. He said if I had a rod, he'd give me bait – he had cockroaches in a container beside him. It was easy to get fishing gear from the PX.' John and his mates managed to secure the oddest of things from the American supply stores. 'Sure enough, the old man would give me a cockroach as bait and we would sit there for hours fishing. At the end of the day I would give him some of my catch. A woman who cooked for me prepared the rest. Made a change from rations. I had to stop though, I was warned off.'

John was clearly enjoying the memory and I did not want to spoil the moment by quizzing him so I never found out who warned him off. He had other stories about his interaction with the Vietnamese people. After seeing the way he communicated with local people on our travels through Indonesia and other Southeast Asian countries, these stories didn't surprise me. Posted to the headquarters of the Australian Force Vietnam, he was based in Saigon. For someone of his disposition, it was natural that he would communicate in a friendly way with people he encountered in non-violent situations. Food was one of his favourite topics and I could imagine him launching into conversation with Vietnamese people relying heavily on tone and body language. While he was there he developed a love of Vietnamese cuisine and culture. In Melbourne when we ate in Vietnamese restaurants, as we frequently did, or walked through the Chinese/Vietnamese supermarkets, he would often refer back to his first encounter with a particular vegetable or food or style of cooking in Saigon.

But even as he spoke of seemingly normal encounters between a local and a foreigner in an exotic land, I knew that he was not giving me the full picture. Several times in the months after we met, he had woken up shouting in fear or anger at something or someone; occasionally I could make out words and they seemed Vietnam or war-related. But he would never explain them. While I was in Papua New Guinea, I borrowed a university library video copy of a multi-part series on the Vietnam War. I was in love with a man who had been involved in the war and I wanted to know more about it. We watched it together; it began with the French colonisation of the country and moved rapidly through the events leading up to the conflict that escalated with the deployment of United States combat units in the 1960s. There was a heavy emphasis on the history of Vietnam and its people throughout the series.

At first John reacted much as I did, with the usual interest and curiosity that one accords a good documentary. Then he began to get upset. 'Why didn't they tell us any of this before we went? We knew nothing about the back-ground or the history of the country.'

As the programmes continued, covering the complexity of the war, depicting the terrors suffered by the Vietnamese people, the convoluted politics, the deaths on both sides, his upset grew deeper and a look of something like horror settled on his face. Even in that early stage of our relationship, I knew that there was something wrong. I suggested that we had seen enough but he wanted to watch the whole series.

'I never knew any of this, I want to see it all,' he insisted.

We made our way through the lengthy and unforgiving documentary series.

'We were told nothing about the country or the people,' he said periodically. 'We were up there doing a job.'

Whenever images of large numbers of South Vietnamese soldiers were on screen, he became particularly distressed: 'If you think we had it bad,' he would say, 'those poor buggers . . .' and that was as far as he could go before being overcome by emotion.

Towards the end of the series, he seemed to move into a place where he was blaming himself for something. I could not understand this.

'You were soldiers,' I said. 'Whatever about the rights and wrongs of the war, you were doing your job.'

'No, no, you don't understand,' was as far as he would go in discussion. At that point he would vanish into himself.

I knew enough to know I did not and could never understand. On the one hand he spoke with genuine warmth about the people he encountered in a friendly way, on the other he was a soldier in a war zone where every local person was the potential enemy; I had no idea how anyone was supposed to reconcile that in their own minds, yet it had been hard to understand why he should be blaming himself. In 1998 Bernard Clancy, a colleague of John's who had also been based in Saigon in 1968–69, published a novel called *Best We Forget*. 'If you want to know about my tour of duty in Vietnam, read that book,' John had said. The book described the strange lives of the desk-bound army staff in Vietnam during this period. Derogatorily referred to as 'pogos' by the rest of the army, these men lived and worked mostly in the city. *Best We Forget* describes a war involving extreme boredom interrupted by moments of extreme danger, but no direct combat.

Tedium, senselessness and craziness dominate the lives of the characters in the novel. One passage refers to a Vietnamese woman who was badly injured, 'just another victim of the war which wasn't really a war but which killed and maimed people anyway, almost it seemed at times for the hell of it, turned others into vegetables and made hundreds of thousands into refugees, homeless, beggars, without self respect. *Sin loi* [sorry about that].'

Best We Forget did not explain John's nightmares but he would not discuss it. 'You're only cleared to rumour,' was his inevitable response to any questions, which I took to undestand that he was not going to give me any solid information. He told me he had worked in the morgue in Tan Son Nhut airport for a brief period; that may have explained his increasingly extreme reaction to dead animals by the side of the road. On a few occasions when he was in the angry part of a mood swing, he would fire off a graphic reference to a mutilated body. I also knew he had been in close encounters with the immediate aftermath of explosions that killed many local people but he would not tell me any more than that when he was awake. And, even if I could make it out, I learnt to consider anything he told me when he was asleep as unsaid.

John was more open about another series of stories; these related to the reaction of Australians to returning veterans. The Australian anti-war movement was similar in style to that in America. There were massive marches on the streets, continued political lobbying by various groups, small groups that openly supported Ho Chi Minh and the North Vietnamese, and a sector that deliberately targeted the soldiers serving in Vietnam.

'We didn't mind the anti-war marches,' John told me several times, 'but some of the lads received cruel letters containing lies about girlfriends and wives back in Australia; and somehow the Ho Chi Minh crowd managed to frank messages onto our mail. We were told not to wear uniforms when we got back to Australia but in 1969 it was hard to hide with a crew cut and distinctive tropical tan.'

The look on his face always turned angry and tense when he referred to this period. There was one story that I had heard a few times: 'I met these two girls, students, on the Manly Ferry. They chatted me up and invited me to a party. Turned out they had only invited me to be the floorshow for their student mates. As soon as we got to the party, the girls announced that I was just back from Vietnam. Those student bastards called me every name in the book. I was so close to punching their lights out but that's what they wanted, they wanted me to lose control to prove themselves right. But if I learnt one thing by the time I left Vietnam, it was how to walk away from a fight. Besides I was outnumbered. I had to back out of that place, for God's sake. But really I was lucky,' he would usually add. 'I was still in the army, which gave me some kind of protection on a daily basis.'

Sometimes bits of this story merged with more traumatic references when he was talking in his sleep but awake or asleep, the pain and hurt of this encounter with the students never left him. I often wondered if the women's behaviour had somehow forced upon him a sense of personal responsibility for everything he said, did, saw, smelt or encountered while he was serving with an army in a war. Was this the extra element that had pushed him over the edge?

*

Although John needed the camaraderie of his mates on Anzac Day, it was the one day in the year I dreaded. John reverted to the mindset of a twenty-year-old in a war zone and became strangely unpredictable. His emotions were all over the place, he got angry very easily, he cried, he drank far too much but showed no signs of drunkenness, and roamed around town with his mates with his medals on his chest and a pocket full of money. One year he petrified me by not turning up until 6.30 a.m. the following morning. After that, he arranged that I pick him up at the pub where his unit met after the march. 'And take me away even if I protest,' he said each year. 'Just get me home.'

Seeing him in the bar at about 3.30 in the afternoon with his mates was another insight into the world of the veteran with unmanaged post-traumatic stress. Once, when I went to pick him up, he looked like he was about to hit a bloke on the far side of the U-shaped bar. I had never seen John get physical when he was angry but this Anzac Day, he was glowering at a man with a cold, unflinching look in his eyes I had never seen before. It took him a while to register I was there, then he clicked into his usual charming self and settled down without a backwards glance to the target of his glare.

Another year I arrived and he was listing his catalogue of health problems to a fellow veteran.

'Why don't you get a Gold Card,' his mate suggested. 'Everything you describe sounds stress related. Go to a shrink, get it declared that you have PTSD – post-traumatic stress disorder – and Vet Affairs will pay your medical expenses.'

'I don't need a shrink, there's nothing wrong with me,' John snapped. 'Think I can't handle it?'

'No, mate,' the other veteran said gently; he was obviously used to wired responses from fellow veterans. 'It's just that that is the only way to do it. You have all of the physical signs of PTSD and deserve to have the government pay for the treatment. But you do have to see a shrink to get the documentation sorted.'

John went to the psychiatrist his mate recommended. As far as I could gather they spent a lot of their sessions talking about four-wheel driving and fishing; it was hard for me to identify any positive impact arising out of these sessions. By now John's sleep patterns were becoming more disturbed. For as long as I had known him, his usual pattern was to fall into a deep sleep around 10.00 in the evening and be up singing and full of energy at 6.00 or 6.30 in the morning. Now he was waking during the night, having night sweats and more frequent nightmares. His approach to food and alcohol was becoming more destructive, his stress levels seemed to be going up but all the doctor could do was increase his medication. Indeed, it was hard to know whether the visits to the psychiatrist were having a positive or negative effect.

By 1998 John had the 'White Card', a lesser version of the Gold Card but it gave him free medical attention and supplies for all of his stress-related illnesses.

*

By mid-1998, I was becoming concerned about John's reaction to the city. He would get uncharacteristically ratty in traffic or with unruly social behaviour on the streets. At weekends he often sat silently looking at the birds in our paved garden or playing with our four Siamese cats, two of which he had bred. Sometimes I would catch him staring into space with tears in his eyes. There was no pattern to this and it never lasted. By evening he would be himself again, ready to join friends in the Bach Hy, our favourite Vietnamese restaurant in Footscray, or go for a stroll down by the bay and on to the nearby port suburb of Williamstown for ice cream. His city stress levels were eroding even the long-term relaxing value of our trips to the desert.

'If we win the lottery, we can keep a place in the city and move to the country,' he said at the end of a working day in August 1998. 'All I want is a piece of land I can call my own where no one can bother me, where I can have an orchard, a veggie garden, a few animals and can make food. I could retire there when I'm fifty-five and you could go on working if you wanted to – or you could write full-time.'

The idea of a country property had taken over from the earlier ambition of sailing around the world but the desire came from the same source – an isolated geographical space where he would not have to interact with anyone.

'How much do we need?' I asked innocently. I had heard this all before and decided it was time to act.

John listed the detail of his fantasy life while I did the figures.

'If we sell our house,' I concluded. 'We'll have enough to buy a country house and half a city apartment; we'll easily get a mortgage for the rest. We don't need to win the lottery.'

John reacted with enthusiasm. 'We could get a place close enough to Melbourne, live there at the weekends and prepare the gardens and the orchard so that when I retire in five years' time, you could either commute to Melbourne or work locally, and I can be a cottage farmer.'

We sold the house, bought the sixty-acre property in the mountains 120 km east of Melbourne on a commuting route, and got a mortgage on a city apartment. We had settled there by Christmas 1998.

Initially it was glorious. John was happy, the place was beautiful and it was like being on holiday. John decided to commute to Melbourne on a daily basis; it was just over two hours door-to-door but he enjoyed the train ride. I stayed in the Melbourne apartment every second night; John stayed in the city only when it was absolutely necessary.

A couple of months after we moved to the farm, we were sitting in the warm air on the veranda in the dusk. It was a Friday night, traditionally a night for total relaxation, a bottle of wine, a takeaway and nothing much else. John began to doze on my shoulder as he often did. Then he began to talk – as he sometimes did. He was tormented. I couldn't make out what he was talking – or rather muttering – about. It seemed to be about combat and death in Vietnam. Deep sobs punctuated half-sentences. Next day I followed up on the more discernible words. As well as being curious, I hoped that if he could speak about the memories that were torturing him, he might be able to release some of his demons.

'Who said anything about that?' he asked suspiciously, when I referred to some of the words.

'You did, that's what you were talking about last night.'

'No way, I would never have said anything about that, you're making it up.'

This scene occurred several more times within the first six months of our being on the mountain. The farm had been his dream and – I believed – his last hope of finding relief from his torment. It was then I realised that the move to the farm was not going to rescue him from his demons and I would never get a coherent understanding about what was feeding them.

*

Some aspects of living on the farm continued to be wonderful. John relished being a weekend farmer. He developed the vegetable garden on organic lines using deer manure to fertilise the beds. The property had previously been a deer farm and there was a high-quality manure/hay mix around the former location of the feeding troughs. John also stocked the chicken coop – or chook yard as it is known in Australia – and spent many happy hours talking to the hens, chickens and ducks, feeding them and collecting their eggs. He bought Nelson, the thoroughbred farm dog: 'Every farm should have a good sheep dog,' he announced having researched the breed. He got some old sheep. 'No point in getting young animals. We can practise on these and give them a good home for the last years of their lives.' And he stocked the dam with fish. The dam was a favourite place for us to sit. It was a 30-ft-deep lake surrounded by enormous gum trees. The previous owners had created it as a back-up water supply but we had no need for the extra water and used it for leisure only. John had a plan to build a jetty into the water but that never materialised.

I loved walking around the property; it was like having the side of a mountain to ourselves. It took a minimum of forty minutes to walk around the entire farm but a leisurely stroll could easily take a couple of hours. We never saw the western boundary of the property, it was buried somewhere in dense, ancient rainforest. Hundreds of exotic tree ferns grew under the canopy of the tall trees; some of the ferns were so old that they had fallen over and had started growing upwards again, giving their soft trunks the appearance of a snake about to strike. A waterfall ran over the rocks deep in a forest in one part of the property. Out in the paddocks, I found a knoll on the top of a steep rise where I could look at the theatre of forest stretching into the distance around me. It was heaven on earth.

*

But John's internal distress was growing. He had uncharacteristic mood swings and would snap for no apparent reason. At first I put it down to increased spirits consumption. For as long as I had known him, he had been a drinker. He would drink wine most evenings, light beer at weekends or when we were on holidays, and whisky or malt as an occasional drink. If he had too much alcohol, it would not be evident until he suddenly fell asleep. At parties, he would keep going, seldom showing signs of drunkenness until he got into the car or taxi and fell fast asleep. His pattern shifted in about 1997 and he began to drink more whisky and malt. Until then, a bottle of either would last for months, now it was only lasting for weeks. By the time we got to the farm, his whisky and malt drinking had increased steadily and it would take him only two or three weekends to finish a bottle of the spirits. If it was a long weekend, he could get through most of a bottle in three days. Unlike beer or wine, the whisky seemed to make him especially cranky and morose and I manoeuvred it insofar as I could to avoid having spirits in the house.

His physical health was also deteriorating. The number of pills he needed to control the symptoms of stress continued to rise and in July 1999 he was given the Veterans' Gold Card, a more comprehensive version of the White Card. This declared that he had post-traumatic stress disorder, or PTSD, and entitled him to a tax-free pension, travel and other concessions and, of course, free medical treatment and medication. There was a pronounced deterioration of his state of mind after that. John recognised it and talked about a relationship between the Gold Card and suicide.

'By saying I have PTSD, they are suggesting that I can't cope and that I'm depressed. I don't like that at all. I'm not depressed. It's just my body is rejecting me.'

In August 1999, there was an article in a Melbourne metropolitan newspaper about three veterans from one sub-branch of the Vietnam Veterans Association who had killed themselves during the month of July just after they had received pensions from Veteran Affairs. The article did not specify whether they got the Gold Card or the full TPI – which declared the veteran Totally and Permanently Incapacitated due to war-related illnesses. John was still working and did not want to be declared TPI. The veterans who died in July were all roughly the same age as John. The sub-branch president speculated that they had died partly because of the difficult process involved in proving that stress illnesses were war-related. Presumably they had gone through the gruelling process John had gone through and which he had been on the point of giving up several times.

I wondered now whether he would have been better off not bothering with the Gold Card at all. But who knows? By that stage, he was on a mountain of stress-related pills every day, so perhaps it was right that the government was paying for them.

*

One Saturday evening in July 1999, seven months after we moved to the farm, John had a pronounced mood swing. He got angry about something and left the house saying he was going to drive away and kill himself. I pleaded with him, trying to calm him down, to stop him, but he only became angrier. He drove off into the dark. The road down the mountain from the farm was treacherous with sharp turns and steep drops into gullies and fields. He was an excellent driver but in the mood he was in, he could easily have driven over the first steep drop and ended up in a mangled vehicle. He had never done anything like this before.

As he vanished into the night, I rang Mary in Ireland in desperation. Never before had I asked for help in a crisis from anyone in the mistaken belief that it was 'not done' to call out for help. Mary, however, had visited me in Australia in June and we had talked at length. As a therapist, she was able to get right through to my version of taboo emotional topics. More particularly I found I was able to talk to her without triggering off any of my own subtle defences, which would have shut me up quickly.

'John's gone out to kill himself,' I told her over the phone that evening. 'He's driven off in the car. It's pitch dark. I wouldn't even know how to go after him.'

Mary calmed me down, using a firm tone and getting me to talk.

Fifteen minutes later, I saw the distinctive headlights of the big four-wheel drive turning into the house. 'He's back!'

'OK, be calm with John when he comes in. Make him tea or whatever but don't try to discuss what has just happened. Ring me later if you need to.'

John looked so sad when he came into the house. He said nothing and went straight to bed where he fell fast asleep. I held him tightly that night; I felt he was dying.

*

That was the first in a series of similar incidents. I rang his psychiatrist to find out what I could do. He did not agree that John was suicidal and said there was nothing to worry about. He put John on Prozac and told him that I had rung. John was furious that I had interfered; I was devastated that the psychiatrist would land me in it like that; I had rung only out of concern. It meant I would not be able to contact the psychiatrist during any future crisis with John after that.

Not long afterwards John overdosed on sleeping pills and Paracetamol during the night. He had been on the farm by himself while I stayed in the city apartment. As usual I rang him first thing in the morning to chat. He did not pick up the phone. I tried his mobile but it was outside the network's range. I waited until 8.45 a.m. and rang his office. There was no sign of him and they had heard nothing from him. That was unusual. I rang home again, repeatedly. Eventually John answered. His voice was slurring badly.

'I think I overdosed,' he said. 'I don't know. There are empty packets on the table, I was dreaming, I feel terrible.'

We worked out he had taken about twenty-five sleeping pills and most of a packet of Paracetamol. I rang his doctor to check if he was in danger.

'Get him to hospital immediately and hope it is not too late,' the doctor sounded a combination of cross and sympathetic. He knew John well. 'If he has taken that much Paracetamol, his liver is in danger. He'll have to get to hospital to have it drained out of him so let's hope it hasn't reached his liver yet.'

I rang the local hospital to arrange for an ambulance to pick him up and got the next train to the hospital.

'I didn't mean to kill myself,' he said, reclining on a trolley looking quite well but slightly apologetic. 'You know I wouldn't do that. I didn't even realise I had done it until I had trouble waking up; then I saw the empty packets.'

I believed him.

The emergency doctor was wary; he stood by the bed with a clipboard. Could John be committed somewhere if this young man thought John was a danger to himself? I was out of my depth on this.

'What happened?' the doctor asked. It was as a good an opening question as any.

'I wasn't trying to kill myself, if that's what you are thinking,' John replied sharply. 'I was dreaming and must have taken the pills.'

'What were you dreaming about?'

'That's none of your business!' He virtually shot up in the bed, now full of energy and in control.

The doctor looked slightly startled and left; we didn't see him again.

'I'm really sorry this happened, I'd never do that to you,' John repeated when we were alone. 'You know I wouldn't kill myself.'

He never told me what he was dreaming about either. His dreams were beyond anything I could imagine. Once before I had seen the power of his dreams. It was shortly after we had arrived in Australia and long before post-traumatic stress was ever mentioned. John had prepared dinner for friends in our house and it had been a great evening of conversation, food and wine. Then, on cue, John had fallen fast asleep on the sofa after dinner was over. Our friends, well used to this, continued chatting around him. Later, when they were going, Ian, a big, tall man, gave John a rough masculine hug to wake him up and say goodbye. Within a split second, John had turned Ian upside down and had him pinned to the floor with his fingers on his throat. I had never seen anything like the look in his eyes before – he was serious. Seconds later, John realised where he was and who was on the ground.

'Mate,' he said, 'don't do that, don't do that. Sorry, I was dreaming.'

The cheerful mood was quickly restored but it was now clear to me that John went to some dangerous places when he was dreaming. After that I was always careful to wake him gently.

Shortly after dreaming his way into an overdose on the farm, John rolled the four-wheel-drive bike accidentally, broke some ribs and refused to go to hospital. He had to be dragged to hospital several days later, again by ambulance, in terrible pain and with his lung now seriously damaged. He was there for nearly a week but recovered his good humour quickly.

'They said I can have a drink with dinner,' he announced to a nurse. 'Is it OK if my wife brings me in a hip flask?'

'I don't believe you, who said that?' she looked at him with friendly suspicion.

'The doctor who was in here a few minutes ago; said it wouldn't make any difference to my lungs.'

The nurse eventually agreed that John could have a single glass of wine with dinner.

*

Life settled down again after that so it was a shock when he rang me one weekday evening for a bizarre conversation. It was about 10 p.m. I had just finished the evening shift in the Library and was relaxing in the city apartment. He was at home on the farm. There had been a television programme on earlier that evening about Australian Vietnam veterans returning to Vietnam to confront their past. It had been several years since John would watch a Vietnam War movie or documentary so I was a bit surprised that he had looked at this.

'When you get home, I'll be hanging from a tree close to the gate with a sign hanging around my neck saying it was your fault.'

I thought he was joking, his voice sounded normal enough.

'You think I'm joking. I'm not. By the time you get home, I'll be half-eaten by the worms. Maybe I'll hang myself around the back of the barn so I'll be nearly all eaten by worms before anyone finds me.'

He went on in this vein for forty-five minutes. He sounded lucid and deadly serious. Nothing I said would divert him and I had no way of getting back to the farm. The last train left at 8 p.m., it was 120 km to the farm and even if I could have got a train, there was no public transport up the mountain. A taxi might have been possible but prohibitively expensive even if I could have found someone to drive that distance. Then my phone battery began to run out. John was now sounding tired. He hung up just as the battery expired. I would have no way of knowing his fate until next morning but I was figured he was too sleepy by now to organise his own hanging.

Next morning, I rang him from a phone booth. He was cheerful, having been out collecting the eggs from the chook yard. He was going to work from home that day.

'But all the things you said last night . . .'

'What did I say last night?'

'About you hanging yourself, about worms and signs . . .'

'What are you talking about, love? I don't remember talking to you at all. I probably fell asleep watching the telly before you got home.'

Another complete blank. I had been awake most of the night worrying about him and he had no recollection of the conversation.

*

In October 1999, exhausted from all of the stress, we went to Phuket in Thailand for a simple, relaxing, two-week holiday. Our visit coincided with an annual vegetarian festival and the place sounded like a war zone with hundreds of firecrackers going off day and night leaving a layer of smoke over the city. John's mood swings went into overdrive. I suggested we leave Phuket but he wouldn't hear of it. One minute he was threatening to jump out the hotel window, shortly afterwards he was chatting in high good humour with the woman at a roadside food stall while she stir-fried jumbo-sized prawns for us.

I was pretty miserable and spent a lot of time in the water at Patong Beach jumping through the waves.

'How much more of this can I take?' I said to the waves. 'Can I live like this, with John's moods swinging all of the time? Can I live so close to someone who can become so angry without warning? This is not a life. I can't sleep. The stress is too much . . .' I had a complaint for every wave.

Suddenly I got a sense that my brother, Mike, was around. Mike had been to Patong Beach in 1977. He had taken a year out during his five-year architectural degree and mounted a successful art exhibition in the Project Arts Centre before spending seven months or so travelling around Australia and up through Southeast Asia. Phuket had been on his itinerary.

'Of course you can handle it,' I imagined Mike saying to me.

Often since 1984 I had dreamt of Mike but I had never had any experience with his memory like this before. This was new and I did not care if I was making it up. My self-therapy sessions in the sea were critically needed.

The waves got bigger and my complaints got bigger. At each wave I thought of an issue, jumped, twisted, then faced the next one without losing my footing. 'That's that problem dealt with, I can manage it,' I thought as I stood waiting for the next one. It was mesmeric and no one, not even John reading on a lounger under an umbrella, knew what I was doing. I felt Mike was somehow involved in this process, challenging me and showing me that I was quite capable of handling everything that was now facing me in my life. Over several days I began to believe that Mike might actually be there helping me. I moved the conversation away from me and onto him. I did not sense any response. The waves had begun to ease. I was running out of complaints but still feeling miserable. Suddenly a big dose of self-pity ran through me.

'It's all right for you,' I said crossly and irrationally. 'You're up there and out of all of this . . .'

The next thing a tiny wave grabbed my feet and turned me upside down into the water. It felt like the rugby tackle Mike used to practise on me when we were kids. I also sensed a sharp retort, 'How dare you!'

I resurfaced, admonished but laughing. 'OK, OK, OK, I asked for that. Total self-pity. But good one.' I was very impressed at how, after four or five days of facing ferocious waves, a gentle swell had rugby-tackled me in no uncertain terms.

The whole encounter with the waves and my imagined or otherwise conversation with the spirit of Mike left me feeling much stronger.

'John is really suffering. He is very difficult to live with at times but he is also ill,' I told myself. 'The mood swings are a symptom of something seriously wrong. I should be looking after him, not snapping back.'

*

We had a New Year's Eve party in the mountains to celebrate the millennium. Warren was there and at one point I saw John talking intently to him with his arm around Warren's shoulders. It was quite unusual for John to have an intense conversation with a man and I wondered what it was about. 'Good bloke,' was all John said when, ever nosy, I asked him. I was constantly on the lookout for someone who might be able to get through to that part of

John where the demons lived. He was so good at presenting a strong, confident face in public, I even believed he had his psychiatrist fooled. Would Warren be the person who could prompt him to face his demons and let them go?

'John was asking me to look after you, keep an eye on you,' Warren told me much later. 'He said that if anything should happen to him, he was glad I was around to be a friend to you.'

That was touching – very touching and very strange. John had quite traditional views about the role of husbands and wives and would not have willingly encouraged another man to support me. He was also wary of my male friends so to talk to Warren like that was very trusting.

John's mood swings continued, varying in intensity and frequency. His body was now in a dreadful state. He barely got a full night's sleep, moaning and crying in his sleep, then having terrible night sweats and waking up. As a result I did not get a night's sleep unless I was in the city alone. Yet I believed his problems could be eased if he gave up alcohol, ate properly and got counselling. I wanted him cured, I wanted my husband, John, back again.

*

Anzac Day in 2000 fell at the end of the long Easter weekend in April. We were driving up the Murray River doing research for *River Tracks*.

'We'll take the extra day and carry on down the river,' John said in Swan Hill.

'But you'll miss the Anzac Day parade in Melbourne if we do,' I replied. 'We have enough material for the moment and this is close enough to Melbourne. We can come back another time and finish it off.'

'No, we're here and we'll carry on.' He was adamant.

The year I don't get rosemary on Anzac Day is the year I'll die. He didn't say that this year.

'I'll get you some rosemary from one of the local parades,' I offered, trying to sound casual.

'Don't bother.' He meant it. I resigned myself to his decision.

*

In May 2000 I went with him to his liver doctor. The doctor spoke in a way John could hear and told him he would be dead within a few years if he continued his current pattern of drinking. As a result John cut down on his alcohol intake dramatically. I went to Ireland for my sister Anna's wedding. John sounded very lonely on the farm: he was on the phone every other day but with the pressure of work, he could not come with me.

When I was in Ireland, Noeleen recommended that I visit Maria. I had had several sessions with a woman in Australia who was able to tell me a lot about myself without asking any questions. She had referred to previous lives I had had and burdens I was carrying. My past lives sounded highly dramatic and fabulous but I was dubious: they all seemed too convenient and unlikely. Perhaps they were just examples of the sort of past lives I might have led. Or maybe they were good, generic stories that I could adapt for my own use. Nevertheless, I had found the sessions useful for some self-reflection – which did not last terribly long at the time: life was then far too busy and exciting for much of that.

But there was something about Maria that was quite different. She did not offer any stories but asked me if I had any questions. I floundered, not sure what to ask. A few questions came to mind. Her answers were direct, confident and short. She made highly practical and earthy comments about managing life with John but she did not say much about John himself. Then I lay on her massage table and she made various signs and muttered various prayers over me. I had heard of reiki and wondered if this was a reiki healing session. The hour session had been tight, well managed and highly professional. I hadn't a clue what had happened but I left feeling noticeably serene.

Throughout the middle months of 2000 John's alcohol intake began to creep up again. In September the liver doctor gave him another lecture: 'give it up or else!' So John gave up alcohol completely for six weeks. The mood swings eased a bit but the physical problems and the deep, heart-wrenching sobbing in his sleep continued as before. Often he would fall asleep on the sofa and I would sit on the floor beside him holding his hand. The sobs came from somewhere terribly deep inside him, his face would contort in pain and he would draw my hand into him and hold on tightly. We could be like that for an hour or two. Then the sobbing would subside and he would snore quietly. Inevitably in the morning he would have no recollection of any of this and I stopped looking for explanations.

*

Nelson began showing signs of deep distress around this time. He was a thoroughbred farm dog that we bought as a pup in 1999. In mid-2000 we began to notice occasional, odd behaviour: he would have trouble getting out of a ditch or he couldn't find his way around a hedge. Then he began to chase the sheep rather than round them up as he had been trained to do. In the last fortnight of his life, he had begun to shake or snarl without warning or provocation. We brought him to a vet who prescribed Valium on the grounds that he might have one of several treatable neurological problems. For two nights, John slept in the hay shed with Nelson, keeping him company and looking after him. There was no sign of improvement. He periodically lost power in his legs, bumped into things and shook. He seldom snarled when John was around but just looked sad and lost.

We took Nelson back to the vet. He was in great discomfort by now and she recommended that he be put down. She was not sure what the problem was but she did not consider it treatable. John cried all weekend.

A week later the vet wrote to us. She had been puzzling over the cause of Nelson's illness and had found some material on a website. 'I believe your dog was suffering from a disease of the brain that prevented him from processing messages,' she explained. 'Over time this builds up and means that the brain cannot process everything and at a certain point begins to overload. It is very rare but can affect children or animals. With children it affects them at about seven years old, in dogs it affects them at about fifteen months.'

Nelson had died of an overloaded brain.

*

With Nelson gone, we went on another two-week relaxing holiday in October 2000, this time to Bali. In retrospect, this holiday was like a heavenly aberration, an oasis in a dark period that ended in John's death. For two weeks we enjoyed being tourists in Southeast Asia once more. We went into markets, John discussed produce with the stall-holders, we tried fruits, dates, vegetables and anything else that was offered. He began drinking wine and light beer again, but in moderation. We swam, ate lobster on a beach, watched stunning sunsets, visited temples and so on, all the usual stuff of a romantic tropical holiday. For fifteen months, life with John had been so difficult that I was beginning to wonder if the man I had married still existed. The fortnight in Bali left me in no doubt but that he was still in there under the trauma, illness, pain and mood swings. The real John resurfacing for a brief period before his death was one of the great gifts he gave me as part of the lead-up to his suicide; it must have taken a massive effort on his part.

The restored pattern of normal, relaxed behaviour established in Bali continued back in Melbourne for a week and I was feeling optimistic about the future for the first time in over a year. We went to Chinatown and took our time over yum cha, met friends in the Italian restaurant strip on Lygon Street, had lunch in John's local sushi bar and tasted some interesting wines. Then, two days before my birthday in early November, I arrived home expecting to find John finishing his own day's work. He was slumped in a chair at the end of the veranda; his eyes were closed and the book he had been reading was lying awkwardly on the ground. I could get no response from him and thought he had had a stroke. I was dialling for an ambulance when he began to snore. It turned out he had been drinking whisky and he had bought me a bottle of vodka.

*

That was the beginning of the end. For the last month of his life, he was in hell and he brought me with him. He fired off round after round of the high-powered rifle. Once, sitting on the front veranda, he fired off twenty bullets into the empty goat shed some distance away, leaving a series of small entry holes in one side of the inverted V-shaped roof and large exit holes in the other. At each explosion, I looked out expecting to see blood splattered over the thin rippling glass of the nineteenth-century hand-blown windows. On other occasions he walked around the property, firing the rifle, the shots echoing up from the valley and each one suggesting that I might have to look for a badly damaged dead man somewhere in the bush.

He slept and woke at the oddest of times, I did not get a straight sleep on the farm for that month. My own anger and frustration with his behaviour was now diluting my compassion. Every time I returned to the farm after work or shopping, I wondered what I would find. Would he have shot himself in the house? Would I have to look for him in the bush? Would I ever find him if he went deep into one of the forests on the property? I had made it clear on the night of the vodka incident that it was his choice but I did not think he needed to kill himself; professional help was available and there were therapies he had not tried yet.

At the beginning of December he woke up very angry with me.

'You're leaving me,' he said accusingly.

I was half-asleep. 'What?'

'You're leaving me. I saw it in a dream. I know you're leaving me.'

'Love, I have no intention of leaving you,' I tried to assure him but, in truth, I did not know how much more of this I could take. I did not feel any sense of physical danger but sometimes his mood swings were so bad, he looked as if he could stare at me, then blow his head off without warning. The fear of that was exhausting. The day before he died he told the police he was suicidal because I was leaving him – at least that was what was in the coroner's report. I wanted to say that he had died of an overloaded brain but didn't quibble, what was the point? It was a nice, neat tie-up for the police – 'wife leaving him, chap shot himself. QED'. It would have taken too much energy to tell the whole story.

*

In November 2002, nearly two years after John's death, I wrote and wrote. Warren was there early in the week and eased things by taking me out for dinner and just being around. The rest of the time I was alone, working through the last eighteen months of my life with John. I stopped at the moment he shot himself. It had all been said, every detail, everything I could be ashamed of – or proud of – was out there in the open, nearly 70,000 words of it. It had been aired and was never to be read again. The only person around to judge me was myself. Had I been complicit in his suicide? Should I have any guilt? Was this why I have been going through such physical and mental contortions? Had I been avoiding facing some sort of guilt for nearly two years? Had I been deluding myself that John's death was right at some level?

The writing process spread out every decision and every response I had made over those eighteen months and placed them in context. I had done my best to live with a man who was being eaten alive by his demons despite his great personal strength. For some time I had been drawn in to help carry some of his troubles but it had been an impossible position to maintain. I had swung with his moods, responding with love and with anger. When I responded to his anger with love, I had nothing to rebuke myself about. But when I responded to his anger with anger, was I letting a dying man down? Even if I had not known he was dying, was it a shameful way to respond to a situation that was life-threatening?

No, I could not think so. All of our responses had been natural for who he was and who I was. Going back over the eighteen months, I had made decisions and responded to

John in the context of the moment. I had handed him back all of his own power that night when I refused to give him the bottle of vodka. If I had not done that maybe we could have continued for a while. Maybe if he had held on he might have found a way to address his demons.

But I never really believed that, not immediately after he died, not now after I had exposed all of the suppressed memories of those eighteen months. John was much too strong a person, far too self-aware and self-determining for me to believe that he had not exhausted all the options that suited him. The damage had been done a long time ago, perhaps in his childhood, perhaps in Vietnam, perhaps when he returned with the other veterans to Australia, or perhaps it was a combination of all of these. Who knows? I do know that he had tried everything that suited him to avoid the violent end; moving to the farm, giving up alcohol and finally holding on to me were his last hopes. And it had not been in my power to save him. Ultimately he made his own decision, just as he had done at every critical stage during his lifetime, and I respected him for that.

24

A NEW RELATIONSHIP WITH JOHN

The purging of memory and experience of the last eighteen months of John's life was a watershed. Something tangible and weighty left my system and I could feel myself physically straightening up. The current of miserable emotion that had been dragging me along for nearly two years had either eased off or I was now able for it. I left me with an urge to take charge of my life once more.

If I had believed that John's death was the complete end of John, I might have been very angry with him. I may have been angry that he had developed post-traumatic stress in the first place, angry that he exacerbated his problems by drinking too much alcohol and eating carelessly, angry that he did not explore every possible avenue of help, and angry that he had killed himself and left me to create a new life alone. It is possible that any sympathy I might have had in understanding his trauma and his deep distress, any appreciation I may have had for all the work he did in trying to tackle his problems would have been consumed by anger at my own loss. And I probably would have been angry with myself for the way I had handled the situation.

But I did not believe that John's death was the complete end of him. Following my conversation with Maria just after he died, I wholeheartedly and easily accepted that John's death was the end of him as a physical, emotional and thinking person, but not the end of him spiritually. In simplistic terms I could see his life as a 53-year stage in what is probably a long and colourful spiritual journey. During this lifetime, for whatever mystical reason, he had gathered a brutal set of emotional traumas that he would not or could not deal with and I could never know how heroically he had tried to ease the impact of his internal torment on those around him. As time went on, I think he was disappointed his body would not allow him to die with a socially acceptable heart attack or organ disease. So in the end, unable to take any more, he shot himself.

In a strange and illogical way, I felt his style of death suited him better than a heart attack. I believe he would have hated the idea of losing control over his last breath; autonomy was critical to him and the idea of doctors being involved in managing his death would have been abhorrent to him. He had died of terminal depression in a most unambiguous way. He had enjoyed a lot of his life; he had brought joy and love into the lives of people around him; he had displayed his depression openly and pushed it to the limits; he had undertaken conventional therapies and demonstrated how ineffective they can be; in the end he was exhausted with this world and decided to leave. Small details of his final journey to death left me in no doubt that part of him had managed the situation beyond a conscious level: everything from shooting at the goat shed to show me the impact of the bullet on his own head, to ensuring that I could hear him but not see him indicated a level of control that his conscious state of mind belied. He had left me with no blame, no trauma and no outstanding questions, which was quite an achievement for someone in the terminal stages of depression. Now, in wherever spirits go or whatever spirits do, he was free of all of that earthly stuff to move on.

Well, nearly free. My homeopathic experience suggested that he still had work to do after his death but there was no point trying to understand what that meant. As far as I was concerned, John was where he should be. When I remembered the young faces of the suicide victims displayed by the White Wreath Association outside the State Library in Melbourne three months after John died, I wondered how it had happened that their depression had evolved, obviously or discreetly, to the point of consuming them so thoroughly that they made the decision to quit this lifetime. While I could not compare the circumstances of John's death to the overwhelming bafflement and loss evident in the commemoration outside the Library, the tragedy of suicide displayed in the posters helped me to recognise how much punishment John had been prepared to endure as he caved in internally. It also emphasised how fortunate I was to have no questions so I could respect John's last decision unreservedly.

My massive slide into the depression of grief was part of my own journey. John would have known that I did not have enough wounds to lead to terminal depression unless I chose that path. He knew that I had a diverse collection of personal and professional support around me to help me through the quagmire and he also knew me well enough to anticipate how I would – or could – react to the challenge.

Sometimes life with John had been like an emotional boot camp at which he had tested my strength; I am confident that he believed I was ready for everything that grief would throw at me when he shot himself. For two years I had faced the challenge and pushed myself to the limits a few times. Fortunately I had the advantage of age, experience, a curiosity about the spiritual dimension and wonderful personal and professional resources to help me.

Of course, none of this was a particularly rational way of looking at my situation but it suited me. However nutty and escapist it might seem to incorporate the spiritual perspective with the human perspective when considering John's death and my handling of grief, there was something quite exciting about it also: if life and death were on a single continuum with veils screening the view beyond my own mortality, then this very big-picture approach was ultimately the only way to address grief. It added an uncharted dimension to my decision-making. It also provided a conscious link to the indefinable feeling deep inside me that was forcing me on by maintaining a detached perspective. And it allowed me to respond to professional people like Maria, Brenda and Vince, who had been helping in very practical ways, yet who all incorporated a much broader view of the world in their work. The challenge was how to incorporate this big-picture version of the world into my own life without losing touch with an earthy reality, where the prospect for fun, laughter joy – and feeling normal once more – resided.

25

ENDING OUR MARRIAGE

John's second anniversary passed quietly with the help of several small ceremonies. My allocated two years of heavy-duty grief were over and mentally I was ready to fire a rocket under my life and get moving again. Yet to my intense frustration there was still a part of me that had no intention of budging and, while I wished to be livelier and more engaged in the world, I remained doggedly attached to my protective routine. Clichés about grief ran around in my head, taunting me: I wanted to believe that after two years I should 'be over it' and 'be getting on with my life'. What was taking my recovery so long? Was I perpetuating my grief for the sake of it? Mind over matter, I muttered as I walked on the beach. Surely as an intelligent person I must be able to put my mind to it and 'snap out of it'. Yet I felt as if I were missing something, as if there were a magical door that, once I pushed it open, I could indeed snap out of this perpetual state of grief. But the magical door remained elusive. It was most agitating.

Once again Mary spotted the problem.

'Cath, how often are you seeing your therapist?' she asked one evening on the phone.

'I suppose every four to six weeks although I haven't actually seen her for about six weeks now.'

She urged me to find another therapist who might help me move on from my current position. I approached Cath Carter, a therapist who had worked professionally with Brenda. She arranged a meeting to see if we could work together.

'What do you want to achieve?' she asked.

I felt emboldened for a second.

'Alignment of my mind, body, spirit and emotions,' I responded, quoting a concept I had come across periodically in self-help books although I had no idea what it meant in real terms. The books, however, referred to such an alignment as if it was a genuine, achievable state of being. In fact for some time I had felt that all of me was not contained in the same physical vessel; when I was lying in the bath or in bed, I often got the feeling that parts of me were floating outside my body. I wanted to put myself back together again but I had no idea how to express this desire in a more lucid way. Fortunately Cath Carter did not seem to find my objective strange.

'Good. We'll start in the middle of January. Here is a list of my conditions,' she said, handing me a page outlining our mutual obligations. I felt immediately safe with her level of control. 'And sometime before we meet, please fill out this sheet. It asks questions about what you are looking for from these sessions and it will help me structure our work.'

I was delighted: Cath was a woman after my own heart. She wanted me to write a performance plan with specific objectives. It was a tough call given that 'total inner peace' is a pretty nebulous concept but if it was to be achievable at all, a plan had to be a good place to start. Besides it was just the challenge I needed at that moment. I was disappointed that I was still a basket case after two years; I was also reluctant to allocate another year to intense grief and simply hope that it would sort itself out. Working towards identifiable goals gave me a sense of control, which I needed to move forward. I had no idea whether identifying and achieving objectives would ultimately help me to end this debilitating grief but it would at least be interesting to isolate and understand behaviours, responses and neuroses that had emerged after John had died and design objectives to try and address them all.

*

I went to the desert for the new year to mark the occasion and think about the future. It was the height of summer and potentially fifty degrees Celsius in the shade but my itinerary was not dangerous. I choose the outback mining town of Broken Hill as my base. It is over 800 km north of Melbourne but the road is sealed all the way. John would have driven it in about nine hours; I took two days. The drive was easy enough; there was activity around the towns en route but other than that the road was almost empty. By glorious chance I found a place that offered cabins on the edge of the desert outside the town. It would have been foolish for me to camp alone in that heat and, anyway, fifty degrees is not comfortable without a nearby river and occasional recourse to air conditioning.

The cabin was one of ten in a group and the remainder were unoccupied. The kitchen was well equipped; the sitting room had a sofa and television, and the bedroom was spacious. It was fully air-conditioned. The sheltered veranda was furnished with chairs and a large wooden table and looked out over the dark red landscape, which had a thin smattering of scrub ground cover typical of this region. There was a low hill with a few trees and rocks on the horizon but nothing else to disrupt the smooth curve of Planet Earth. This was a luxurious way to be in the desert and I had a week to experience it.

I sat and walked and read and slept and thought. At night it was pitch dark with no back-light and no moon; there was not even a glow coming off Broken Hill. I used a couple of lights in the distance and the stars to navigate my evening walks to and from the cabin. A spectacular electrical storm broke a couple of days after I arrived and the temperature dropped to a comfortable thirty degrees. Two years before I had sat on the veranda on the farm feeling completely peaceful but not connected to earth. Once again I was sitting on a veranda looking out over a stunning landscape but this time I was definitely on earth because even in this beautiful place I could not be completely still and content: my body was sore and my mind, fed by edgy emotion, was running overtime. Nevertheless, if I was going to address my grief in a practical, forward-looking way, I could not find a better place in the world to attempt this.

*

Fundamental to the way I approached this challenge was to try and work out what an end to grief might constitute. I had tried this before without success: the only logical conclusions that I could envisage were death or a new romantic relationship. No matter how laterally I tried to think, I could never imagine a different, more satisfactory ending that was within my control. Yet occasionally I sensed that there was another way to end grief. It was so elusive that even when I got the feeling, I could never hang onto it for long enough to define it. All I knew was that there was great strength in the sense; there was also great excitement around it, as if there was a whole new way of being open to me if I could just keep going. I wished I could identify what the sense or the new way of being was so I could make plans, but then again – I could almost hear the desert laughing – if it was that new and significant, it was not going to be something I could plan for.

The only plan I could make was to have faith and see if working with Cath Carter would make a difference; she was offering an opportunity to extend my self-awareness using methods she was comfortable with and it was up to me to make the most of it.

Sitting on the veranda, I casually browsed *Simple Buddhism*. Suddenly a single line jumped out and triggered a significant shift in my attitude. Quoting the Noble Truths of the Buddha, the authors stated 'Life is suffering', 'Suffering is the doorway to deeper insight' and 'You can end suffering.' I had already accepted that my pain was commonplace but this was the first time I had fully registered the idea that I could end the pain. Suddenly grief – or its manifestation – was no longer something that had been imposed on me; it was not some foreign body that had landed in hideous circumstances on top of me; it was not an alien to be fought off or fled away from; instead I began to see that the grief was an integral part of who I was and the more I understood this aspect of my being, the more I could explore it, understand it, ease it and ultimately transform it. I was reminded of the time when my body was twitching uncomfortably to the thousand boxing matches under my skin and Brenda helped me to take an interest in the sensation by feeling it before it disappeared. Whatever convoluted way my mind was working, the Buddha's Truths had instantly changed my attitude; it was not going to reveal the elusive sense of future adventure but it would help me move into the next phase of the current adventure.

In an attempt to gain insight into the difference between a state of mind dominated by grief and a state of mind that I could characterise as normal, I summoned up memories of scattered moments of pleasure or absorption that I had experienced since John's death. These moments included my focus when navigating my nieces around Paris, the flashes of insight, joy or physical steadiness encountered during guided meditations, the light-heartedness I had felt when I completed a session with Maria in Dublin, pleasures such as watching an Oscars ceremony with Warren and Garry in the mountains or being engrossed in a book or a film, the bursts of hilarity with my family or friends, the blankness of sleeping, and the warmth of feeling John around me when I picked rune stones from the bag. During those times, I had been swept along by the activity and there had been no evidence of the anxiety, fear and self-consciousness that permeated so much of the rest of my life. Perhaps, I reasoned, the challenge was to increase the percentage of time in which I was absorbed and, by extension, decrease the periods of anxiety, fear and self-consciousness. If, by some miracle I could add joy and warmth to the mix without joining a religion, turning into a complete crackpot, dying or grasping at a new relationship just to escape the pain, then maybe I could achieve a viable end to grief and feel normal once more.

Whether it was the atmosphere of the desert, the promise of an exciting future or a determination born out of weariness and frustration, this fantastical idea felt like a real possibility. I had a lot of confidence in Cath Carter's skills to guide me and, after two years of therapy and self-analysis, I believed it was possible to dissect every aspect of my life in order to rebuild it. Besides I had isolated myself from normal social activity for so long that I had nothing to lose by spending another year behaving oddly, so long as it seemed to be heading somewhere useful.

*

During one of my walks in the desert I decided in principle to end my marriage to John. When the time was right I would take my rings off but in the meantime I would start thinking in terms of being single again. In dark moments, the prospect of staying married to John until I died was tempting. I could keep him in my life as a constant reference point, talk to his memory in bed at night, imagine I was discussing decisions with him, and keep him close to me until I died.

In enlightened moments, the destructiveness of staying married was obvious: I could not take up the challenge of completing my voyage through grief if I stayed attached to my marriage. It felt a bit cold to end it but it had to be done. In *Simple Buddhism* the authors refer to the impermanence of life in the Buddha's Second Noble Truth; the world is constantly changing, they say, and 'attempting to hold on to things is like trying to grasp and hold air in your hand.' My marriage was like air and letting it go willingly and gently in the Australian desert had an elegance that sat well with my new determination to expose, work with and ultimately end my grief.

26

EMOTIONAL SPRING CLEAN

Therapy with Cath Carter matched my expectations. The weekly sessions were focussed and purposeful and it became easier to isolate specific aspects of grief under her guidance. The most distinctive manifestation in my case continued to be emotional overreaction and endless conversations running around my head about ordinary, everyday encounters or events. Cath drew on the same techniques as Brenda to help me stop this chatter by identifying what was my business and what was someone else's business; it continued to amaze me how effective this process was in dissolving a troubling story from my mind. Better still, I found that I was now able to use these techniques at home with reasonable results.

The next challenge was to stop the chatter from starting up again and once more I headed back to obscure childhood events to locate the trigger for my responses. The power of unresolved issues from childhood to have a profound influence on a person's life is routinely spoken about in professional therapeutic circles. Brenda had touched on this but now, as my own self-awareness deepened, I began to take a more active interest in the theories and how they were affecting me. Although there had been nothing startling or newsworthy about my own childhood, it seemed that the ordinary, everyday pressure on a child trying to find space in a large, busy family could leave unresolved emotional issues lurking deep within the psyche. Yet as each emotional pattern was therapeutically excavated, I wondered at their source: it was hard to believe such ferocious arguments in my adult head could emanate from such a simple episode as exclusion from a game of football when I was three. Nevertheless I was thankful that Cath did not spend hours trying to talk me through rational explanations of the patterns; instead she encouraged me to feel the old emotion briefly, then help me to let it go.

The impact of this work was unmistakable and within months I began to notice that I was sleeping more easily and was generally much calmer. Despite this my body began to react strongly and, without warning, I developed an inexplicable abhorrence of meat. Potatoes and other heavy foods were also causing an uncomfortable reaction so Vince put me on a cleansing diet for a few weeks: I liked to think that the spring clean I was doing on the invisible parts of my being under Cath Carter's guidance was being reflected in a spontaneous spring clean in my physical body.

*

One of the powerful techniques that Cath used was to provide me with a method of working directly with my emotions. It is a well-known therapeutic process and it involved me sitting opposite an empty chair and imagining my emotions were sitting in that chair. Under Cath's guidance, I would ask the empty chair a clear question – which initially felt a bit weird – then move into it and respond to the question. The results were very curious because, once again, I gave unexpected answers and even used words or phrases I would not normally use. Until this point, I had had a limited view of how I might be feeling about anything emotionally. The only emotions I had been aware of before now were the ones that caused inconvenient physical reactions, such as sadness that led to tears, anger that led to feeling wound up, embarrassment that led to blushes and conversations in my head, confusion that led to stress in my head and body, and irritation, frustration, anxiety and lots of ill-defined fear that led to general discomfort. They were all the standard emotions of normal living and I had managed them successfully for years; they had just become extreme and unmanageable following John's death.

Now here was an opportunity to understand all of these as well as get at more subtle emotions, the ones that did not have obvious physical side effects and could therefore be ignored indefinitely. I was constantly surprised with the range and power of my responses whenever I was speaking from the emotions' chair. At times during these perform-ances my head would admonish me for being self-indulgent or sounding like a bit-player in a Woody Allen film. At other times my head would nod wisely to itself and refer back to concepts of emotional intelligence and emotional maturity mentioned in self-help books. Whatever my immediate response, it soon became clear how, in subtle ways, unidentified emotions had been restricting my progress and no amount of thinking or rationalising was going to 'cure' these emotions. Cath did not stop to analyse and I did not ask her to. We let my emotions have their say and moved on.

'There's an awful lot of unspoken stuff in there,' I said to Cath after one gruelling session. 'How on earth will I ever be able to clear it all?'

I really wanted to stick the nozzle of a vacuum cleaner into whatever constituted an emotional vessel and suck the whole lot out.

'You are on the right track now,' smiled Cath optimistically. 'The task is to let these emotions be heard, acknowledge them and then release them.'

I took her word for it, although I was pleased when she followed some of these sessions up with bodywork not unlike the work Maria did; her hand movements, invocations and other actions gave the impression that she was indeed wielding a vacuum cleaner. At a level that did not bear close examination, I felt the work was somehow sucking out old, weighty and tiring debris.

*

As a Transpersonal Counsellor, Cath used other surprising tools in her approach to counselling.

'It would be useful to explore your history using your astrological chart,' said Cath one day. 'I'll prepare it before next week and we'll take a few sessions to go through it.'

I had always been attracted to the notion that planets had an impact on my life. If we are energy and the planets are very powerful energies, it makes sense that we would have some sort of relationship with them, however marginal.

'The alignment of the planets at any given moment is fact,' explained Cath. 'It's a question of how their impact is interpreted that makes them relevant in this work. We all know that the moon affects the tides; we can also detect a different mood in the air during a full moon if we stop to pay attention. A crowded restaurant on the night of a full moon, for example, would not be an easy place to work. But be aware that the interpretations I give you about the impact of planets in your chart are my own. And remember that regardless of what the planets are doing, your life is the consequence of personal choice and self-determination, not fate.'

The chart was so detailed that it took several sessions to relate and discuss. As a tool to work through every unbalanced bit of myself, it was remarkable. The astrological summary of my life to date matched the real summary of my life to an extraordinary degree. There was no way Cath could have based most of this on anything I had told her; nor was I squeezing my life into the patterns presented. Periods of pronounced – and therefore memorable – joy, sadness, pleasantness, success or misery appeared to coincide with periods of major support or what is referred to in astrological circles as challenge from the planets. Occasionally Cath would focus in on a specific few weeks in the past and ask what had happened during that time; usually it was a low point in my life but sometimes it was a highlight. Simplistic clichés about the characteristics of people born under different star signs were irrelevant: the chart and reading were much too detailed for that. Periodically, however, Cath would smile at a response and say, 'That's a very Scorpionic response'; this was a reference to Scorpio, the birth star I was born under and the perception that Scorpios enjoy exploring transcendental concepts.

At a practical level, incorporating astrology into my self-exploration allowed me to relax and take a generous overview of the story of my life so far. Awkward, unpleasant, embarrassing or difficult memories became easier to accept because now I could regard them as identifiable steps on a productive journey. There was no suggestion of fortune telling in this work either; retrospectively it simply presented the planetary waves that had supported or challenged the course of my life to date. Whether I was responding to planetary influences or whether the energetic waves from the planets exaggerated whatever was happening in my life, I could not tell and it did not matter: as far as I was concerned the astrological influence was marginal anyway. As a tool for the future, I would now keep an eye out for potential planetary influences coming through because, so long as an interpretation did not interfere unduly with my decision-making, I could see only value in taking the opportunity to ride with them. Life was tough enough without trying to buck the energetic waves coming off the planets as well. Besides, given the blank-canvas nature of my life at that point, forthcoming astrological waves of support might give me a few ideas as to what I would do with the remainder of my life. It might even prompt me to take some interesting risks.

*

While I was working with Cath, I undertook a three-week beginners' counselling course in Melbourne. Although the course was designed as the introductory stage of the lengthy education and training that led to a professional qualification, my interest lay in understanding more about the system that had been supporting me for two and a half years. Much of the training involved undertaking several ten-minute counselling sessions with class members in which one student was client, one was counsellor and one observer. Initially, when I was client, I made up problems, fearful either of giving too much away or of terrorising an inexperienced classmate. Yet I desperately needed to talk because the nature of the discussions during the day was stirring up a whirl of agitated thinking. Midway through the first week, however, other class members broke the ice and revealed real problems during these triad sessions. I decided to join them and use the ten-minute sessions to talk about exactly how I was feeling at that moment, which of course included aspects of my own story. Even after so much therapy, the power of downloading pent-up chatter in my head in these contrived counselling relationships surprised me: it was like expelling air from a pressure cooker.

None of the students ever discussed what they had heard during the ten-minute sessions, it was as if the words spoken during that time had not been shared. Sometimes – often – personal stories came up in conversation over tea or lunch and we chatted about aspects of those stories as one would during any intensive training course. But even here the content of the conversation was not augmented by any additional information released during the triad sessions, nor did information revealed informally during tea-time chats enter the ten-minute sessions; it was remarkably easy to confine the content of a formal session to the allocated ten-minute period. It demonstrated very clearly to me the difference between talking to a friend about a problem and talking to a counsellor. As a result it also validated an early realisation that my friends were not and could never be my counsellors; conversations with friends would always be markedly different in style and content to conversations with professional counsellors.

27

MEMORIES OF IRELAND

While the work with Cath Carter moved ahead, it also became critical that I should get some movement into my life outside the therapy room so I applied for a job in an international library in the Middle East. Although professionally it was perfect, it was the ready-made expat society in an exotic location that really interested me. While I waited for news, the idea of leaving Australia took root and I became more convinced about the attractions of continuing my life in another country. Two months later, when the rejection letter arrived from Egypt, I was amazed that the standard pang of disappointment was quickly followed by the startling idea of returning to live in Ireland. Not once in eighteen years had I thought I would ever live in Ireland again; even during the depths of grief, living in Ireland had not been an option. Yet somehow this letter had transformed itself into an invitation back to my homeland.

Although I could feel the power behind the idea, it was hard to believe it was what I really wanted. Using techniques I was perfecting, I became still by counting my breaths in order to consider the idea without distraction. Was it real? Was it a consolation prize coming out of disappointment? Was this where my grief had led me? Was it the inevitable result of John's death? I ran the objections and doubts through my head and was surprised and pleased when none caused a reaction. What about living in Ireland? Could I stand the weather? Could I risk living on a small island again? Might I get stuck there and never be able to escape it again? Could I even afford to live in Ireland? The country was nearly twice as expensive as Australia. As I conjured up each objection, my breathing remained steady and there was no clammy fear running around my head or up my veins. The concept of returning to my home country seemed to suit me and, as I thought about it more, it became quite exciting: it was a new challenge in what was effectively a new country to me. Ireland had changed so much during the eighteen years I had been away that I couldn't presume to know it; at the same time, my family and several old, close friends all lived there so they would ease the stress of settling into an alien society.

*

Before I flew out to Papua New Guinea in 1985, life in Ireland had not been all bad; in fact by Irish standards of the time I had been very fortunate. I had graduated with an arts degree from University College Dublin in 1979 and worked in temporary positions before getting a job in the National Gallery library in 1980. Librarianship had been my chosen career and the Gallery job was ideal but the salary was at the lowest grade in the civil service. Nevertheless I had been lucky to get a job at a time of high unemployment and even luckier that the job had been interesting. The Gallery had given me nine months off to do the Library Diploma in UCD in 1983 and, in 1985, I was offered a position at a professional salary in the Dublin public library network.

By that stage, however, Mike was dead and my outlook on life was depressingly bleak. The bathroom wall in my four-room flat was damp, yet I was grateful for the place because the flat was spacious, the bathroom was not shared and I could keep my bicycle in the hall of the house. Even on a professional salary such flats would have continued to be my only option for a long time; tax rates were very high and there was little hope of saving a deposit for a mortgage without a miracle. Driving lessons and a car had also been a fantasy, so walking and cycling in the rain, or waiting helplessly for a bus had been the only options. Foreign travel had been a rare treat, air fares were astronomical and a week in the sun usually required the help of a bank loan.

At a broader level, the country had been pretty miserable too. The Catholic Church had dominated society and politics for decades, the economy was in a dreadful state, tens of thousands of people were emigrating, the situation in Northern Ireland looked hopeless, and a group of senior politicians in the south were providing a steady stream of entertaining but ultimately depressing gossip about their corrupt and hypocritical behaviour.

'Why did you put up with it?' Australian friends used to ask after hearing stories of life in Ireland.

Why did we put up with it indeed?

But in fact we didn't; with careful management, lateral thought and lots of cynicism, it had been possible to create tolerable lives and circumvent the more intrusive aspects of Irish life. By 1985, however, I had had enough and grabbed the opportunity to work in Papua New Guinea. I left with one suitcase, fifty pounds, a one-way ticket and a letter offering me a job; I had no credit card and no personal contacts; if anything had gone wrong, I would have been in serious trouble but the risk was worth it.

I was one of an estimated 28,000 who left Ireland in 1985. It is hard to believe now but even in the 1980s, there was still a trace of the unspoken perception that emigration was like a death. We had been raised on the melancholy images of the generations of Irish people who had been forced to leave Ireland in the past with only the extremely fortunate ever managing to see their homeland and relatives again. In Melbourne it was easy to empathise with the many descendants of Irish emigrants who were looking for their roots through the Genealogy Centre in the State Library. I had remained in constant contact with my family in Ireland and visited on average every eighteen months to attend weddings, christenings, communions, birthdays, conferrings and a book launch. As the price of phone calls fell and email became available, communication became casual and commonplace so, despite the distance, I always felt part of my extended family; nieces and nephews, who had been born after I left, knew me nearly as well as if I had been living down the road.

By 2003, the concept of emigration in Ireland had changed completely. Hordes of young Irish people were taking working holidays in Australia for a year or two. They presented an image of adventure and challenge rather than loss and exile. 'People don't emigrate any more,' an Irish twenty-something told me. 'We just live abroad for a while and we'll go back to Ireland when it suits us.' I had also been 'just living abroad' but I had remained fearful of living back in Ireland until this moment. Now, about to go home, I decided to tap into the young, optimistic mood of contemporary Irish travel abroad and find a framework for considering my move to Ireland as the continuation of a seamless adventure through life rather than the unfortunate end result of the death of my husband.

*

In the spirit of adventure, I decided to increase the odds of a new life and leave my library career when I returned to Ireland. Lots of self-help books talked about putting oneself in the hands of the universe and they often included short, inspiring tales of someone in a depressing place who left their partner, job, home, or lifestyle and found happiness with a better partner, job, home or lifestyle. 'Ask the universe for what you want and God will provide,' the books recommended. Despite my cosy relationship with the spiritual world, I knew there would be several years of tough work between leaving Australia and whatever fabulous future the universe could rustle up. But if I could stay my course, keep my nerve and respond enthusiastically to situations as they arose, maybe life could be exciting once more. It was worth the risk. Besides if I could consider John's life as part of a much bigger spiritual life, then it was time I considered my life in the same vein.

Viewing a whole life in retrospect is, of course, much easier than trying to view it from inside a particularly torpid phase but the astrological approach helped me to make this shift. Forcing a change of direction professionally in my mid-forties felt right when I took a broad overview of my life. I did not know how I was going to earn enough money to live in Ireland but I believed I would be grateful for this decision in a few years' time. My values had changed and I was now prepared to work in a shop and live simply if that meant developing some other part of myself; I had enjoyed libraries but I was not convinced that I would learn much more about myself if I stayed with them. On top of that I was in the rare situation of having no responsibilities at all and this made it virtually imperative that I make a daring decision about my future.

*

With no job or plans, it made no difference when I arrived in Ireland so I used a meditative visualisation to help me pick a date. A remarkably strong image appeared: it was of Ireland as a flower closing in for winter and everyone closing in with it. A second image appeared: it was of a flower in spring opening up again and everyone rising out of it full of intentions and busyness. It was a strong and lingering image, just like a vivid dream. As I thought about it, it seemed perfectly logical. There is a lot of calmness about winter with plenty of routine and long dark evenings to talk. Summer on the other hand suggests considerable movement, mixed activity and travel. For someone returning home with the intention of rejoining the community, it seemed like a good idea to arrive at the beginning of the hibernation season despite the onset of awful winter weather. My decision on the time of year was made.

Cath Carter checked my astrological chart to identify dates that would provide planetary support for the move. An October date fitted well so I tested the power of the universe by seeing if I could use my frequent-flyer points to get a business class seat to Dublin via Japan on that date. I anticipated that the flight would be upsetting so it was the perfect opportunity to use seven years of accumulated points, travel in luxury and visit a country I had never been to before. By chance – given the short notice in frequent-flyer terms – the airline was able to provide me with exactly what I asked for. Even with my new desire of being a rational woman living in the real world, I was rather pleased this unscientific approach to moving country had fallen into place. But just in case I needed a reminder not to put too much faith in astrological charts, my flight was cancelled and I left Australia a day earlier, which happily gave me an extra day in Tokyo.

28

LEAVING AUSTRALIA

'You'll be back,' a surprisingly large number of people said when I told them I was leaving Australia. They all seemed to know an Irish emigrant who had gone back to Ireland, then returned to Australia. The reasons for the round migrations varied.

'Her children couldn't settle into an Irish school. They were all born and bred in Australia and to them Ireland was a foreign country.'

'She really wanted to be near her family in Ireland, he really didn't. They lasted a year and came back.'

'They couldn't get decent jobs and gave up in the end. Even moving twice having sold everything the first time, their standard of living here will be higher than it could ever be in Ireland.'

'One of the kids became quite chronically ill so they returned to Australia, the care is much better here.'

'Her husband went to Ireland to see if it would work but he decided they couldn't afford to live there so they're staying put.'

And so on. As soon as my decision became known, the stories kept coming. I had heard a few stories over the years but never suspected that there were so many of them. The amount of change involved in moving country was daunting anyway but perhaps managing a family group of three, four or five people through the process proved too much. I only had myself to worry about and had no fear that I would reverse my decision: it was time for my life to move forward; staying would have been to retreat. But it was salutary to note that the journey might be tougher than I anticipated.

*

In July, on the nineteenth anniversary of Mike's death, I went to Uluru, or Ayers Rock, to say goodbye to Australia: the sacred Aboriginal site and national landmark seemed a fitting location to do this. While I was there, I had a strange experience. I had moved away from the crowds to an isolated desert place about 3 km from Uluru. Given the flat desert landscape, I might as well have been alone with the extraordinary rock. Uninhibited now about talking to myself out loud and confident there was no one about to hear me, I thanked Australia for everything it had given me: the friends, the deserts, the homes, the jobs, the publications and especially the years with John, which had been the best years of my life.

Next thing I got an unmistakable sense of disembodied voices saying 'You have been a very welcome visitor to Australia, but you will never belong here.'

Instinctively I looked around, even though I had just sensed the voices rather than heard them. 'Your feet will never take root here, you will always walk above the ground in Australia,' the message continued. Instantly I envisaged my feet walking about twelve inches above the ground.

As far as I was concerned, the Australian spirits were talking to me. Getting a sense of unseen forces in the Australian desert is not unusual but the personal nature of this message made me feel massively privileged. 'You have been a very welcome visitor . . .', the words lingered, '. . . your feet will never take root here.' There was no arguing with that; if I had had any doubts about the wisdom of my decision to leave Australian and return to my homeland, this message from whatever source eliminated them completely.

*

The stopover in Tokyo was a perfectly distracting break between two lives. By the time I had negotiated my way around the city and through the obscurely illustrated menus in small restaurants, I had no time for self-pity. After the three-day break, I relaxed in a luxurious window seat looking out over the tarmac waiting for take-off.

'You're safe now, love, you're on your way home,' a message came through my head without warning.

Before I even had time to register the meaning of the words, tears poured out of my eyes. It was so distinct. I knew it was John.

'You're safe now, love,' I replayed what I had heard.

'John, are you here? Is this the end?' I tried to keep my mouth still. His message seemed to have a definite ring of finality about it.

'Champagne, madam?' A head appeared over the screen that was giving me a level of privacy on the plane. It was a steward. 'Oh, are you all right?' he added seeing the state of me with mascara running down my cheeks. If he had heard me talking to myself, the flow of champagne en route to London might have been restricted.

'Fine, thank you.' These guys would be used to over-wrought passengers, I reasoned. 'Champagne would be perfect.'

As soon as the screen was back in place, I toasted John with every ounce of melodrama I felt. My marriage was over and so it was time to release John from being an integral part of my daily life. After making the decision to end my marriage in the desert on New Year's Eve, I had waited for the right moment to take off my rings. One day some months before I left Australia, I had removed my rings and, with a simple ceremony, buried them symbolically in a jar of red sand. Yet I had stayed married to him until that moment in Tokyo Airport; from now on I would incorporate him differently into my life. I landed in Ireland as I had left it, a single woman on a fresh adventure.

29

THE RETURNED EMIGRANT

The first months back in Ireland were strange and unsettling and any positive impact about being back among my family once more was eliminated by the sheer stress of moving to a new city. My mind was in two countries, Ireland and Australia. Everything, even the simplest of things, was processed with immediate reference to Australia. I thought in terms of Melbourne when trying to work out where a Dublin street or suburb was – was it in the eastern or western suburbs (in Melbourne terms), or on the north side or south side (in Dublin terms)? It was very confusing.

When the Australian way of doing things clashed with the Irish way of doing things, I had to work hard at keeping my frustration under wraps. 'But in Australia . . .' The useless protest was often on the tip of my tongue as I tried to negotiate my way through yet other tangled aspect of Irish bureaucracy.

'I'll stop saying that after two years,' I promised everyone in answer to the glazed look that came into people's eyes when I started with 'in Australia'. 'But in the meantime please put up with it, I'm all over the place.'

On top of the geographical dislocation, my mind was also located in several different time zones. In Ireland I was in the 1980s and 2003; in Australia, I moved between life with John and life without John. The Australian mixed time zones were not a problem by now – I was used to them – but the Irish emotional flashbacks were disconcerting. Walking by denuded trees in the grey, damp air, I would suddenly get an unpleasant feeling of being back in the 1980s when life was bleak and the outlook hopeless. It was probably the most uncomfortable aspect of returning to Ireland.

I had no idea whether these flashbacks were a standard experience for returned emigrants or part of the residual grief for the loss of John, or perhaps even a general grief at the loss of my previous life. That I was fragile and easily agitated was unquestionable. All the usual signs had flared up again: the easy tears, sleepless nights, conversations going nowhere in my head, bouts of self-pity and that eerie feeling of not quite being in the real world. But I had no way of telling whether it was simply part of the normal bemusement at settling into a new country or my familiar grief aggravated by significant change. Surprisingly there was virtually no discussion in the media about returning emigrants, their reactions to coming home, and people in Ireland's response to their arrival; yet the Central Statistics Office estimated that 140,000 Irish emigrants had returned to live in Ireland between 1999 and 2004.

After the initial buzz of arrival activity, an uncharacteristic feeling of profound lethargy took over my life. I had been used to taking exhausted downtime when I was in the depths of grief but back then I had an excuse; now I did not feel I had an excuse yet I could not stir up enough energy to be active and functional. All I wanted to do was write emails to Warren, watch *Neighbours* on television, have long breakfasts reading the Irish newspapers, sit on the internet reading the Melbourne newspapers, talk languidly to the neighbour's cat and make unhurried meals. I had no job, no home, no car and my possessions were on a ship on the high seas. I felt like a bored teenager with no ambition, no responsibility, no interest and, although I could see what was happening, I could not find enough motivation to change the situation.

'Buy a phone and a car as soon as possible,' advised Mary. 'You won't survive in Dublin without those. Once you have them you can relax and sort out everything else in time.'

That gave me something to do and by the time I had negotiated the maze of trying to establish myself in a country without a history, local identity or job, I was beginning to sharpen up again. My supportive Irish network found me short-term jobs that forced me into the discipline of getting out of bed on dark, cold mornings and driving to work through heavy traffic to the outer suburbs. I was beginning to feel normal once more.

*

The major breakthrough of my return to Ireland occurred on an isolated beach in west Waterford a few months after my return. I was staying in a cottage that was beautifully situated looking out over the sand, the rocks and the rough water beyond. There weren't many people about and I spent a lot of time walking on the beach in the bright, grey sunlight or sitting on the patio overlooking the water, wrapped in warm clothes, hats, scarves, gloves, blankets and two hot water bottles up my jumper. The sights, smells and sounds constituted a classic Irish landscape; this was beautifully and uniquely Ireland – there could be nowhere quite like this anywhere else in the world and I felt I belonged in it.

On one particularly wild and damp walk I became aware of a question tapping at my mind: 'are you really here in Ireland?' It was a surprise because, at the time, I was entirely focussed on trying to walk while keeping as dry as possible. 'We need to know if you are really back here in Ireland,' the nagging thoughts continued in the first person plural. 'If you are, we'll help you. At the moment you are just like a visitor.' I got a fleeting sense of a crowd of Irish spirits; it was very similar to the sense I had had at Uluru in July but this time it was a body of Irish spirits that seemed to be talking to me.

'Are you really here in Ireland?' The question stayed in my mind.

It was a very good question and one I had not given much consideration to before now. Where was I really? How much of me was still in Australia? How much of me had actually landed on Irish soil? Physically of course I was in Ireland but perhaps emotionally part of me was still in Melbourne. I realised that to be properly committed to a new life in Ireland, I would have to declare myself back in this country sooner or later. There could be nothing casual about the declaration because, once it was made, I would be committing to, and establishing roots in the land and culture I had been so happy to escape in 1985. It would also mean a definite end to any fantasy of resuming my life in Australia. However, hopefully, the declaration would help me accept the migration and reduce my frustration with the differences between Ireland and Australia.

As I pondered the full implications of making a declaration over the next twenty-four hours, it became clear that if I wanted to evolve out of being a grief-ridden person into a light and cheerful person, I would have to do it in Ireland. By now I readily accepted that aspects of my grief were being influenced subtly by thought patterns and responses that were nearly as old as myself. Logically, therefore, I realised that I could achieve a more comprehensive outcome from my grief if I completed it in Ireland rather than Australia because the process of getting there would eventually have to incorporate my entire life.

The only question was whether I ready to declare myself at this point or whether I needed more time. A breathing exercise stilled my mind to allow me to weigh up this decision. As I thought of the declaration, my breath remained steady, the blood in my veins did not race or pound and my body relaxed; it felt right. A brief foray into thinking about postponing the declaration created an immediate tension in my body. The decision was made. I went down to the beach. The weather was even worse. A wet rain lashed against my face, the wind howled, my scarf and coat flapped around me, I felt like something out of a black-and-white 1930s movie. I made my declaration out loud into the wild weather. It felt strangely physical. I was too wet and cold to try and work out if the body of Irish spirits on the beach was responding and I bolted back to the house, my legs below the anorak-line saturated.

The weather was calmer next day and, when I was walking on the beach wondering whether I should do anything to add to the declaration, I got a lovely image of a path being made for me through high grass. I interpreted this as a welcome home. Whatever about the Irish spirits talking to me, psychologically the declaration marked a major shift in my attitude to being back in Ireland.

30

JOHN'S CHILDHOOD AND YOUTH IN ENGLAND

John had known how attached I was to my family and had once offered to live in Ireland with me if that was what I wanted. Considering his history as a child and youth, it was an immensely generous offer but I could not have done that to him – he would have hated Ireland; when compared with Australia, it would have been too much like England for him – small, wet, claustrophobic and, at times, oppressive. Service in Vietnam had only increased his inability to tolerate crowded, stressful places.

*

When John left England in 1963 with the Big Brother Movement, he had no intention of ever returning. There had been a fuss when he had run away from home in 1961, then aged fourteen. According to a local South Shields newspaper report, he had left a note saying, 'Don't worry, Mam, I'm just going to London to work.' The article quoted his mother as saying, 'It's not the first time this sort of thing has happened. Just before Christmas he tried to walk to an aunt's house in Kent.' The article added he was only 4 foot 8 inches tall (he was 5 foot 9 when I knew him).

'I'd run away a few times before,' John told me in Papua New Guinea. 'But this time I was making sure I could stay away. I met a couple of Greek sailors at the railway station who had jumped ship.' He reeled off their names with flourish and great affection. 'They hadn't a word of English but wanted to go to London. I had no money but could help them get to London so we did a deal: they paid my fare and I did the talking.'

Clearly John's skill of communicating in any language using a combination of body language and tone had developed early on.

'I went to my father's aunt and uncle in London. Uncle Bert had worked in the dairy and got a gold watch after fifty years of service. Aunt Kath gave it to me after he died.'

Aged fourteen, John got an apprenticeship in a big London city hotel. In the newspaper article, his mother said, 'He has always loved to cook. We gave him all the encouragement we could.'

'The head chef was a big bastard,' John told me. 'He was Italian, said he couldn't understand me. I had a very strong Geordie accent. He used to yell at me all the time, "I am Italian and everyone understand me, you are English and no one understand you".'

That was not the only problem.

'The head chef was always having a go at me, trying to grope me. One day he went too far and got me between the legs. I went for him with the knife I was carrying. Fortunately it was only a salmon knife and it bent, but I was fired.'

John quickly got a job in a London family bakery and made pastry for a year. Then he saw some posters for Australia.

'Sunshine and fresh fruit and jobs, it looked so different from England. I knew I had to get out of the UK. I had to go north again to get my father's signature. Of course I found him in the club drinking. All he said was "where the bloody hell have you been?" It had been two years since he had seen me but he signed the form without a bother and that was all I cared about then.'

In the 1950s and 1960s, Australia was a popular destination for British emigrants, who were being encouraged with assisted passage schemes; an adult could travel to Australia on a boat for ten pounds, while under eighteens travelled free. However with the Big Brother Movement, John flew from London to Sydney, a journey that involved seven or eight refuelling stops. He had one small suitcase and a St Christopher medal his Aunt Kath had given him. The case with his belongings was stolen in the hostel shortly after he arrived; he was wearing the St Christopher medal when he died. The Big Brother Movement gave him a small amount of pocket money on arrival, which he promptly spent on a pineapple. He settled down once he joined the army. In 1969 after his tour of duty in Vietnam he returned to the north of England to visit his family.

'Where the bloody hell have you been?' his father greeted him again, this time buying him a drink. As an adult drinker and smoker, John could now fit easily into his father's world.

John's father died of lung cancer in 1972.

'I was in Papua New Guinea at the time. I rang him several times before he died but he told me not to come home.' Whenever he related the story of his last contact with his father, he became distraught. 'Not that I could have afforded to but I would have found a way if he had wanted to see me. He just kept saying, "Don't bother, don't waste your money".'

For all the trouble he had had as a child with his father, John usually spoke about him with love. Contact with his mother petered out during the 1970s and, when I met John in 1986, he did not know whether his mother was alive or dead, or where his brother or sister were. Coming from my background of close family, I couldn't understand this and persuaded him – without much difficulty – to spend a week in England looking for his family.

*

In 1987 we visited his Aunt Kath in London first. She greeted him with open arms.

'He was such a scrap of a lad when he first came down from South Shields,' she told me. 'His fists were up all the time ready for a fight, the poor boy. His dad, Bob, was a bright lad but a bit wild, a bit of a black sheep. His family was from Kent but Bob went north to strike out on his own. He was a bit rough with his own. John had to get away from him. Bruised and always ready for a fight he was when he got here, the poor lad.' Kath chattered on; I picked up an image of a small, thin boy constantly on the alert for an attack.

After we left Kath, John and I headed north. The closer we got to South Shields, the more John's accent shifted. He pointed out familiar landmarks in an increasingly Geordie accent.

'How did you lose your accent?'

'I didn't lose it, I dropped it. When I joined the army in Australia, the lads picked on me because of my accent, called me a "pommy bastard". So I got rid of it.'

We drove around neat rows of small, red-brick terraced houses. He stopped outside one. 'An aunt used to live there.'

John went up to the house by himself. This was a nervous moment. From what I knew of John even then, it seemed quite likely that if he did not find anyone there, he would simply leave the area and never come back. He returned to the car.

'The people there knew my aunt. She's moved and they don't know where she is, but they've given me the address of my cousin. She might know something.'

We visited the cousin who was not too impressed. 'Where the bloody hell have you been?' she demanded. 'Your mother hasn't been well. She's had a few strokes. I can give you Caroline's number but don't expect her to greet you with open arms, you haven't been in touch for years.'

John had been friendly with this cousin when they were young. Now she seemed to be quite aggressive. I presumed people would be pleased to see someone who had been out of touch for so long, but apparently that was not the case. The cousin allowed John into the house to ring his sister, Caroline.

'Where the bloody hell have you been?' Caroline cried down the phone. 'It's our Stan. You come straight over, you'll be staying the night with us.'

She seemed delighted to see him and sat holding his hand with tears in her eyes.

'I'm called John now, no one calls me Stan,' John explained.

'You'll always be our Stan, no matter what you call yourself now,' she replied.

John had dropped his first name, Stanley, when he moved to Australia and had become known by his middle name.

'Mum's not bad,' said Caroline. 'She's had three strokes but is living by herself and has no problem communicating and getting around. She drinks Barbican all day – that's a non-alcoholic beer,' she added. 'She hasn't touched the booze for a while. Let me break the news that you're here, I don't know how she'll react and I don't want to give her a heart attack.'

Next day we followed Caroline into his mother's house.

'So there you are, our Stan, have some tea.' She did not seem at all surprised to see John for the first time in eighteen years.

She was sitting in a hot, cosy room, surrounded by everything she needed to make herself comfortable, including a can of Barbican and a packet of cigarettes. She behaved as if John was a regular visitor. John played with her budgies while his mother talked of the wonderful presents she had given her children for Christmas when they were young. Neither John nor Caroline said much. His mother continued to talk contentedly, recounting apparently false tales of past Christmases. Suddenly she paused.

'My goodness. That's the first four syllable word I have said since my last stroke,' she exclaimed, and she sat still for a few moments, lost in the wonder of her achievement. Then she switched her attention back to us.

'Have you contacted our Brian to let him know Stan is back?' his mother asked Caroline.

'Not yet. I haven't been in touch with him for a while. I don't know whether he is in the country or not,' Caroline answered.

'Your brother has done very well in Germany,' his mother told John.

'Brian has served in Germany with the British Army,' Caroline explained. 'He may be there now but he has a house in England. I'll try ringing him from here.'

She got through. He was in England. John and Brian talked. There were tears in John's eyes.

'We're meeting him in a couple of hours at a motorway turn-off south of Newcastle,' he announced to his mother and sister. 'We'd better go.'

John left with as little ceremony as he had arrived and we set off to meet his brother. On the way he said virtually nothing. Brian was waiting when we pulled into the turn-off. The brothers hugged.

'Follow me to my house. You'll stay with us a few nights,' Brian said. 'I want you to meet my boys.'

Brian and John spent several days talking and crying. I heard many stories about their childhood, some funny but many very sad. Brian related tales of the physical and emotional abuse they had both suffered with much of it directed at John because he was the eldest.

'He tried to protect us', Brian said to me, 'and he got a very hard time for it. Dad put him into hospital a few times. Broke his arm twice. Knocked him unconscious several times. Once he pummelled him up against a wall until he slid to the ground. I don't blame him for leaving, he really had to get out.'

Tears rolled down John's cheeks. Brian's recall was much more precise than John's. He remembered stories that John had shut out a long time ago. Brian's wife and I sat in on some of the conversation but most of the time left them to their intense and deeply personal conversations. They parted, promising to keep in touch.

'Make sure he does,' Brian said to me when we left.

John and Brian remained in contact. Eight months before John died, Brian and his wife, Sandra, visited us on the farm in Australia. They talked at length in private. Brian wasn't surprised when I told him John had shot himself.

31

ESTABLISHING ROOTS IN IRELAND

Establishing my own personal space in Dublin was a crucial next step in returning to Ireland so buying a home became my priority early in 2004. Between exorbitant house prices and the loneliness of buying a place without John, the task threatened to be a nightmare. However, now keenly attuned for anything that could destabilise me, I adopted a strategy to turn it into a process rather than yet another unpleasant round of personal development.

The strategy was both practical and a bit daft. Part one of the practical bit involved listing everything I wanted in a home, from two bedrooms and secure car parking, to space for a dishwasher as an essential item; a large balcony and nice views were listed as desirable. The daft bit was to put the list out into the universe and ask a home to be delivered. The people who had bought my farm in Australia had said they had done just that: 'we worked out what we wanted,' they told me, 'and sent the list out to the universe.

Then this place appeared.' My farm had sold so easily that I had been convinced that divine intervention had been involved although the estate agent had just called it luck. In Dublin in 2004 I needed every bit of divine intervention and every scrap of luck to find a home that I could afford, in the area that I wanted, with the facilities I needed, and quickly.

The second practical part of the strategy was to look at twenty properties in Dublin over a two-week period and keep notes on each. The properties only had to meet the essential criteria and be under a reasonable price; precise location and state of repair were irrelevant. This took the emotion out of the search because however ghastly each place was, they counted towards my goal of twenty and gave me an indication of what was on offer.

But after looking at twenty-five properties, it was time to beg the universe to deliver; if I had known of a patron saint of home buying, I would have tapped into the great Irish tradition of lighting candles to him or her at every opportunity. Instead I did a meditative visualisation and got a vivid image of a map of a triangular section of Dublin. The image was strong and remained steady despite my usual attempts to explain it away. After I came out of the meditation, the image of the map remained clear. As a librarian, I had always dreaded an enquiry based on information gathered in a dream or a vision but I had asked the universe for help so it would have been hypocritical of me not to take up on this feedback. I walked and drove through the triangle indicated in the dream-map. I rang every billboard and checked every agent in the area, confident that the perfect home was just waiting for me to find it. There was nothing. The image of the map floated in front of my eyes. I went over the triangle again and on one occasion, to avoid causing an accident by distracted driving, I drove just outside the triangle and pulled into the entrance of an apartment complex. There was a billboard advertising a two-bedroomed apartment. It was too small for my purposes but on the way out the door the auctioneer, who was showing it to me, stopped to chat to a resident.

'He wants to sell his penthouse,' he said casually when he rejoined me. 'Lovely place, he's the original owner, big roof garden. I'll get that on the market shortly.'

By Saturday, the penthouse with the roof garden was mine subject to the usual paperwork. In a wonderful instance of symmetry, the keys of the apartment were handed over to me on 7 April, a fortnight ahead of schedule. John's birthday had been 7 September and he had died on 7 December; the sale of the farm in 2001 had gone through on 7 March and now I was taking possession of my new home on 7 April. It was a pleasing coincidence.

*

Now if only I could find myself in a new, romantic relationship, perhaps the pleasant, calm structure similar to what I had known with John could be restored. I was still experiencing fleeting moments of strength, which held the promise of an exciting future that was not reliant on a romantic relationship but, try as I might, I could not turn those moments into a practical reality. Indeed, if I were being honest, I continued to hold the popular notion that that as soon as a widowed person has a new partner in their life, all will be right in their world once more and everyone can move on, relieved that the sad episode is over. Of course I wanted to complete the challenge of finding internal peace and tranquillity through my own resources but I was also growing weary of grief and isolation and a relationship would have been very convenient. One way or the other, I knew I had to throw off the purple cloak of widowhood and become an active, single woman with a social life.

'Going to Ireland as a single woman is a pretty daunting prospect,' I told Warren just before I left. 'Ireland is such a family-orientated society and the traditional role for a middle-aged widow isn't very exciting.'

'Think of it as an adventure,' Warren advised in his usual, practical way. 'You're single. Just go out and chat up men and see what happens.'

'I don't have the nerve and I was never any good at that sort of thing anyway.' It was too easy to be absorbed by self-pity in the circumstances.

'There are plenty of single men out there and all you have to do is find one of them.' Warren would never buy into my dramas. 'Besides you have already been invited out on a date once.'

'Yes, and John's ashes were still on the bookshelf looking at me.' I groaned. My one disconcerting moment of singledom as a widow had happened six weeks after John died when a local farmer called by to ask me out to a pub in the town.

'Well,' responded Warren, 'you have to give him marks for trying; and it shows that you still have it in you.'

'Oh I don't think so. Anyway I'm probably too old now.'

'Don't be silly. You just have to go out there and practise. If you don't think of yourself as being available, no one will know you're available. So get out there and practise chatting up the men. Don't worry about detail, just do it.'

*

In year four of grief, the question of an intimate relationship was the one that could still reduce me to tears and no amount of fighting, exposing or analysing my emotional state could divert this unwanted response. Nor had I any clue about how to create a social life in Ireland. I was still having difficulty with casual conversation because my reference points always began in Australia. I needed more time to tune into the local social, political, economic and cultural aspects of life that feed normal social discourse before I could even think of reaching out far enough to establish new friends. Even casual references to the weather needed some mental gymnastics on my part: rain in Melbourne is good for the gardens, rain in Dublin is a pain in the neck. On top of this, my style of social conversation was still embedded in the couple combination that had evolved with John over fifteen years. Between everything, conversation was a self-conscious effort. Perhaps because of that, I felt a real temptation to return to the black cloak of widowhood and avoid the pressure of re-entering society at all. After all, now that I was in my own house, I could spend hours vanishing into the intimacy of meditation and the spirit world if I wanted to and I need not be lonely at all. But I also knew that to take that course would simply be an avoidance tactic and, I told myself, cowardly. Besides, I could live for another forty years and I didn't fancy a life of perpetual widowhood.

'We're too old to meet men in a pub or a club,' a single woman of similar age said to me one day in Dublin. 'I'm going to check out Internet dating. Why don't you join me? A crowd of us are going to meet and try it out together.'

There are plenty of successful Internet relationships about and, as a fast typist, it had a certain appeal – single, unemployed, fast typist, looking for meaningful relationship. But my body revolted at the idea before my mind could dismiss it: the threat of encountering weirdos or deceit eliminated any of the potential joy that Internet dating might have for me.

'Get your friends to set up a blind date for you,' suggested another friend. 'It's a very good way of meeting available men and you'll have great fun. If you go out with no expectations, the worst you can do is waste an evening.'

I recoiled at the idea because, for no apparent reason, it made me feel very nervous but if this was the way single people of a certain age meet single people of a similar age in Dublin, why was I resisting these practical ideas? Was I relying too much on the basis that if there was a man out there for me, he would just appear? Was I using widowhood as an excuse not to push out into an unknown and uncomfortable world?

I talked to Maria. She echoed Warren's words.

'The way you are at the moment,' she said, 'you could be passing the man of your dreams every day on the street and you wouldn't recognise him. You are closed off to the idea altogether. Everything about you and your energy is suggesting you are unavailable.'

'What can I do?' I wanted to burst into tears.

'Open your heart and invite people into your home for dinner.'

'I haven't any furniture yet, I'm still setting myself up.'

'Throw a sheet over a couple of boxes and put some cushions on the floor,' said Maria countering the resistance. 'Inviting people into your home is about opening yourself to the joy of other people around you. And it's a good way to start opening your heart to love and a romantic relationship.'

I was relieved with this advice: preparing dinner for friends once more was definitely enjoyable and it allowed me to put the idea of actively seeking dates on hold for the present.

32

INTERVIEW WITH 'THE IRISH TIMES'

In April 2004 *The Irish Times* interviewed me for their 'New Life' feature on the back of the Tuesday Health Supplement. It was an unexpected opportunity to address several latent issues about grief, suicide and my return to Ireland before I spoke to the reporter.

'They're interested in the returning emigrant aspect,' I told my sister Sheila on one of our regular walks. 'The feature is about changing lives but how do I talk about my decision to come home to Ireland without making reference to John's death? And how do I talk about John's death without mentioning his suicide?'

If John had died of natural causes, would the manifestation of my grief have been different? I had no idea but I didn't think so.

'Cath, tell the truth, just say it straight,' Sheila advised. She had worked in the Irish media for a long time and her advice was very clear. 'Don't fudge the story, there's no point in that. The truth is simply that John committed suicide. That's who he was, that's how he died and his death is the reason you came home.'

'I don't mind who knows how John died, that's not the problem,' I answered. 'I'm just not sure if it is too shocking.'

What was the problem? Everybody who knew me in Australia knew John had died and, if they didn't, I presumed they did. It did not matter to me whether they knew the circumstances or not, but it did matter that they knew that he was dead. I remember after Mike died, I appreciated it when someone said something, anything. 'Sorry for your troubles' or 'sorry to hear about your brother' were common expressions. Friends or acquaintances who said nothing at all unnerved me. Did they know that Mike had died? Should I tell them? Did they want to know? Would I embarrass them by telling them? It seemed such a confronting thing to say: 'Sorry, I'm a bit out of it, my brother died in an accident a few weeks – or a few months – ago.' Yet if I did not get even the briefest acknowledgement of my loss, it made it very difficult to relate to the person again.

It had been the same after John died: for the first year or so it had been very important to hear an acknowledgement – any acknowledgement – of what had happened; normal interactions could resume after that. I didn't mind how clumsy the acknowledgement was so long as it was real. Indeed there had been a few bizarre exchanges that had actually cheered me up; one of these was when I was still on the farm not long after John died when a kindly if somewhat nosy neighbour stopped to chat.

'There are lots of stories about what happened,' he said as a greeting. 'I was in town when it happened and received a phone call from an ex-neighbour who said she wasn't supposed to know about it but would tell me anyway.'

I didn't enquire what his ex-neighbour wasn't supposed to know.

'Some said there was a murder here,' he added, looking at me inquisitively – even hopefully, I suspected.

I had expected the mountains to come up with stories about John's death, particularly after the police had blocked the road for a couple of hours – but a murder? It was almost funny but I assured him that there had been no such event.

Not long afterwards, an old acquaintance had passed me in the street when I was standing talking to Warren about something and laughing. The acquaintance stopped purposefully in front of me and stared, her face inches from my face.

'How can you laugh?' she demanded.

It was a startling interruption. Had I heard correctly?

'How can you laugh?' she repeated at close range.

Yes, I had heard correctly.

Dumbfounded, I tried to think of something to say. I knew her question arose out of concern for me rather than any outrage at a recent widow laughing in the street. I also took her comment as her way of acknowledging John's death; it was clumsy but who was I to judge the quality of someone's ability to express condolences? Fortunately Warren restored order by shifting the conversation but every time I thought of the question after that I smiled and every time I saw the acquaintance, I wanted to laugh out loud. On several occasions, memory of her comment acted as a tonic, physically lifting me out of a terrible feeling of flatness.

My need for acknowledgement in Australia ended when I threw off the protection of the widow's black cloak after the incident with the bad-mannered man in mid-2002. From then on it no longer mattered whether someone knew my husband was dead; the need for the protection afforded by general acknowledgement of my troubles had dissolved. Yet for a while after I came back to Ireland, I wondered, at the back of my mind, if someone I was chatting to was aware that I was a bereaved widow. It became a cause of internal conflict. At a rational level it did not matter whether they knew or not, but at an emotional level I yearned for the protection of the black cloak again. Prior to this *Irish Times* article, I had not consciously accepted that this need had recurred so, now that I was aware of it, I could monitor it and let it go again. I also decided that it was a characteristic of grief to be included on my list for future reference; so when I no longer cared – or even thought about – whether someone knew of my widowhood status, I would know I had moved on.

*

The next question in relation to the interview was about how much information I make public. Do I let it be known in a national newspaper that John committed suicide? Would my acceptance of John's decision be creating a problem for people who might be considering suicide? Might it be upsetting for someone bereaved by a suicide? I knew enough about the topic to recognise how delicate and sensitive a matter it is; I did not know enough about it to feel sufficiently skilled to talk about it without creating problems.

'That's the journalist's job,' Sheila said. 'Leave it to her. She knows, or has enough guidance around her, to know how to present suicide in a public forum. Trust her on that.'

'What about my family? Will I be creating a problem in stating in public that their son-in-law or brother-in-law killed himself? What's the stigma level of suicide in Ireland?'

Vague memory suggested the stigma level had always been pretty bad in the past. I don't remember hearing of any suicides before I went to college and even after that the stories were from unfamiliar parts of the country. Inevitably, however, the hook of those stories was that the suicide was not acknowledged as such; someone had died, everyone locally knew it was suicide but no one was saying so out loud. Suicide was a criminal offence in Ireland until it was decriminalised in 1993 but perhaps the most practical reason for fudging the truth was the tradition that someone who committed suicide could not be buried in consecrated ground; if everyone pretended it was an accident then the person could be buried in the local graveyard.

I never really considered other reasons for the source of the stigma; perhaps it was because it suggested mental illness or selfishness in the person who died; perhaps it was a pall of guilt that hung over the person's family and friends; or perhaps it was connected to a religious belief that people who commit suicide are damned. I was fortunate that a combination of John's openness and my therapy had saved me from dwelling on any of these thoughts. Nevertheless in the years after John died, I was at the receiving end of a few negative reactions to suicide from people who were angry with him and perhaps angry with me.

'He was a selfish bastard for killing himself,' was a classically direct Australian comment.

'People who commit suicide are just selfish,' was a less direct comment but probably meant in much the same way.

Occasionally questions seemed to be directed at my role in John's suicide.

'Did you know he was going to kill himself?' Yes, I wanted to say, but I was not sure it was a wise answer without loads of explanation.

'Couldn't you have stopped him?' I did stop him: probably for years longer than I realised.

'Couldn't you have got him some help?' And yes, in so far as I could get him help.

They were all good questions and never upset me but if I had been feeling a stigma around his death, I wonder if those questions may have sounded aggressive.

If someone was important to me, I did not want them to carry anger about the way John died so I related enough detail about his pain to help them understand his decision. But it was weird when someone I didn't know well – or even at all – vented their anger with John and suicide on me. Two or three encounters left me feeling very unsettled but, in these cases, I did not feel there was any need to defend John; I did not think their anger had anything to do with him.

*

The proposed interview with *The Irish Times* raised other issues about how I spoke of John's death outside the confines of family and close friends. It was one thing to be direct and truthful, it was another to sound callous or blasé. I tended to talk matter-of-factly about John's death because it was the truth. This did not take away from its tragic and devastating nature but fudging the truth only created more problems. In fact there was something ordinary about his death for me: I had lived through the lead-up and had no outstanding questions about the actuality of his death. Insofar as death is a part of life and therefore ordinary, John's death was ordinary. The hopelessness, violence and tragedy had created an intimidating set of challenges for me but that was my business. Ultimately John's suicide was simply the way he had died. Yet sometimes I stopped myself talking in that vein for fear that such matter-of-factness could be misinterpreted.

'Just tell the truth', Sheila advised, 'and manage the story around that for yourself. Work out what you are going to say and prepare how you are going to say it. The journalist has only so much time to write a story. If you ramble, she will have to try and work out what you want to say. So keep it simple, go for the truth and place John's death simply in the context of your decision to return to Ireland. That is the story they are after.'

What about the question of branding myself as a widow whose husband shot himself, as one friend had suggested?

'The only person who can brand you is yourself,' Sheila said shortly. 'Just don't do it.'

*

The interview was conducted over the phone.

'How did he kill himself?' the journalist asked at one point.

'He shot himself,' I answered, 'but I don't think you should mention that, it might be too much detail.'

I don't know why I suggested she hold that back. Perhaps it was because it sounded very shocking or perhaps because it was going into territory of talking about suicide in public that could have consequences. It did not matter to me who knew how he died but I did not want to cause unnecessary shock. 'Besides', a friend said, 'it's a conversation-stopper and people will run a mile from you.' Fair point, but if someone asked, I answered truthfully. The alternative was to sound mysterious and evasive, and in Ireland it amazed me the number of people who came straight out and asked direct questions such as why I left Australia, my marital status, John's death, children, and so on. Australians, in my experience, did not do that on the same scale. After honing my casual conversation skills in

Melbourne, I had not worked out how to dodge questions – if indeed questions needed to be dodged. So it usually emerged quickly enough that my husband had died a number of years ago and, after the follow-up question, that he had killed himself. The problem was to ensure that it was not a conversation-stopper and I guess that was all part of learning how to be Irish again.

*

I was very impressed at how well and succinctly the article was written. A few people made kind comments but other than that there was no reaction. It was just another slice of life in a newspaper, a truthful story simply told. The issues it had raised caused me no further anxiety. Better than that, this episode had effectively transferred the whole package of my grief into Ireland; there was nothing remote about any aspect of my story or the story of John's death any more. Any inclination I had had to use geographical distance as a way of separating out and dumping bits of the story to shortcut my grief now vanished. I had no excuse to hide from any of it any more.

33

DEATH OF MY FATHER

My father died in June 2004. He was nearly 86 and died very peacefully at home after dinner one evening. His was such a dignified and natural end to a long life that I felt a real sense of privilege at having witnessed it. Since returning to Ireland in October 2003, I had spent many evenings chatting with him. He talked of his childhood in Sligo and Limerick, his early career as an engineer in Limerick in the 1930s and then in England immediately after the war. He talked of coming back to Dublin and meeting my mother on a mountain walk. He told stories about the evolution of concrete practice in Ireland and about teaching engineers and architects in University College Dublin. His memory was clear and his stories colourful.

As part of the funeral process, he was laid out in the family home where he had lived for over fifty years. People paid him their respects and then joined my mother for a cup of tea. His grandchildren played music around him and we all took an opportunity to talk to him privately. I wrote a short, three-minute summary of his life for the beginning of the funeral mass. This was the first funeral I had been to since John's and I was nervous about it. My sister Brigie, a natural public speaker who could make a menu sound interesting, agreed to read it. The night before the funeral, I sat by my father and talked quietly. He was lying there looking peaceful and dignified.

'I'm sorry I can't read the piece I've written,' I said out loud. 'I don't think I could get through it without breaking down.'

'*Of course you can, dear. Don't be such a drama queen,*' came a silent response.

I blinked. He still lay there peacefully dead. There had been no movement in the room. The statement lingered in my head: Of course you can, dear. Don't be such a drama queen.

Well, the first part sounded like my father, the second part didn't. 'Drama queen' was definitely not terminology my father would have used. Was it me? Was it my father? Was John around? There was certainly a hint of John about the message, he would have had no time for such dithering; but the message also had a ring of the sort of encouragement my father would have given me over the years. Were the dead men in my life ganging up on me? It was well after midnight, my mother had gone to bed and my sisters had gone to their homes. It was one thing to be kooky on my own and with my own late husband, but to start getting kooky in my parents' house with my dead father would be too much.

However I accepted the challenge from whatever the source it came from and began reading the three-minute piece. Before long I broke down. I started again, got through that point and broke down on the next. I kept reading it until I could get to the *Vale* without breaking down at all. In the morning I read it to my mother and my sisters. Words were changed here and there but each time I got through it with no difficulty. I knew I was ready.

His funeral was a beautiful ceremony. The funeral directors expertly held up the traffic in the congested streets around Beechwood Avenue in Ranelagh as we walked behind the hearse from home to the church. After the funeral mass, the cortège drove back to the house and stopped outside for a couple of minutes before moving on to the cemetery; it was all so traditional and Irish and fitting for a man who had lived a long, fruitful life in Ireland. My father was buried near my brother in Deansgrange Cemetery.

*

Besides being exhausted, a bit sore and a little bit jumpy, I also felt remarkably restful as my father's death had been so natural. He seemed ready to leave. His body had gradually worn out, and, as far as I could gather, he had a very easy sense of his own spirituality. Emotionally I felt very much in the moment. There was sadness at his departure from my life, but also joy and appreciation that I had been part of his life, pleasure that I had had plenty of opportunity to chat with him since the previous October and privilege that I had been able to witness such a gentle passing. Initially I was pleased to observe that I was experiencing my father's death without anger, fear or sleepless nights. Perhaps, I reasoned, all of the work of self-exploration I had done over the previous three and a half years was paying off.

Yet a few months later I began to feel waves of overwhelming loneliness. I could not understand it. The pattern of my life had not changed much as a result of my father's death other than to spend more time with my mother. I also felt there was no unfinished business between him and me. Where was this loneliness coming from? It was powerful enough to reduce me to deep sobbing. At times I was wailing almost as ferociously as I had done in the first year after John's death. Once again I could not sleep and conversations were running through my head at ninety miles an hour. I tried to calm down using basic breathing exercises but even these skills were failing me now; I could not achieve any peace. I was displaying classic signs of grief yet rationally there was no reason for this.

'It is so frustrating,' I told Maria at my next session. 'I can't understand it. It's as if I am reverting to my grief of over three years ago. I am genuinely peaceful in every direction about Dad's death. I know he has just gone to where he should be. I am trying to create stories about Dad's death to justify how I am feeling but even they don't fit. What is going on?'

Maria looked at me.

'Yes,' she said after a pause. 'The loneliness you are feeling has to do with John's death. You couldn't have felt this loneliness when John died; with everything you had to face then, you probably wouldn't have survived. Now you are ready to feel that loneliness and your father's death is allowing that to happen. His passing was so peaceful that it enables you to bring back up other grief that hasn't been expressed yet. It will be very hard for a while but if you go with it, allow yourself to experience the loneliness and emotions around it, you will heal your emotions at a much deeper level and you will emerge much stronger than before.'

That made immediate sense and, if I needed confirmation that my grief for John was a mess of old stuff, here it was. Unspoken grief for Mike had clearly been mixed with my grief for John. Now my father's death was stirring up residual issues still lurking about after nearly four years of exposure, dissection and letting go. The anatomy of grief as an accumulation of unresolved troubles from the past took on a new clarity. My reactions to the feelings of loneliness were terrible for a while but once I knew what was going on, I allowed them to happen. I drew on the old reliable techniques of walks, baths, undemanding conversations, fresh food, old movies and so on to look after myself; I did not want to get stuck here but I also wanted to create space so I could be a basket case and take the time to heal. By Christmas the manifestations of troubled emotions had eased off considerably and I was able to sleep properly once more.

34

BREAKING DOWN THE BARRIERS

By the summer of 2005, four and a half years after John died, balance had been restored and life was perfectly all right. I was enjoying being a full-time writer and had little to complain about. Periods of anxiety and fear had diminished and I seldom felt self-conscious or jumpy in company. I was using the techniques Brenda and Cath Carter had taught me to manage most situations and I used the empty-chair technique to tap into my emotions and give them a periodic airing. I could have cruised on like that for the rest of my life but in fact I was actually in danger of slipping into the half-life mode that I had so wanted to avoid. The core of the problem was obvious: any reference to the absence of an intimate, romantic relationship still had the power to upset me, particularly if someone raised the question in kindly tones. Of course I could have lived with this by managing my responses as they arose but the subtle voice deep inside me, which had been urging me along over the previous years, was never going to be satisfied with that.

Fortunately, late in the summer of 2005, Robert, John's son, gave me a push in the right direction in a most unexpected way.

'Hi Cath, can you recommend a hostel?' he asked, ringing from Dublin airport. 'I'm going to stay in Dublin for a few days then head off around the country for a while. Any suggestions?' He was on a classic Australian round-the-world trip and had called into Ireland.

'Stay with me, of course', I said without hesitation, then wanted to bite my tongue off. Under normal circumstances, I would have been delighted to see Robert but no one had yet stayed in my apartment even though I had the second bedroom fully set up. Now I was very nervous about having a visitor in my home.

As soon as Robert arrived, he dumped his bags confidently in the spare room. The tension that took over my body was bizarre and extreme. 'Get out of my house, get out of my space,' I wanted to scream but held my tongue. I was shocked at my response yet the presence of another person in my precious space was unbalancing me. For so long solitude had been my best coping mechanism and had got me through four and a half years of massive change but now it was being invaded. Fortunately Robert did not seem to notice. We caught up with each other's news; I told him a lot about Dublin and suggested interesting places he might enjoy around the country. Occasionally one or other of us referred to John. When Robert drove off to County Clare in the hired car, I was so relieved that I was shaking and it did not take long to work out that there something was seriously wrong with me. I had an appointment with Maria shortly afterwards.

As usual Maria was direct: 'You have put up barriers around yourself and are not letting anyone in; Robert has arrived and is crashing through those barriers,' she said. 'He just wants to see you, find out how you are, talk about his father with someone who knew him and loved him, and spend time in Ireland. And', she added, 'Robert is one of the few people who can break through your barriers. He is closely connected to you but he is from outside your comfort zone. By allowing him into your home and making him welcome, you will find that it will become much easier to welcome other people into your life in the future.'

'But he left his stuff around the place, he sat around reading and didn't take off his shoes when he came into the house; he was doing my head in,' I protested; yet even as I spoke I could feel myself trying to keep invisible barriers in place.

Maria was unmoved. 'That's what young men do, they sit around, leave the newspaper lying on the floor, eat everything in the fridge, it's simply what they do. Catherine, you have isolated and closed yourself down and you need to let people back into your life.' She paused, then took the problem further. 'You know, you haven't had physical contact for a long time and that is like being blind or deaf for all of that time – physical contact is one of your senses.'

I wanted to weep. She had struck the chord that seemed incurable.

'You have done very well,' she went on, 'but this is one big thing left for you to do. You need to waken your physical senses up again. Could you get a dog or a cat?'

That was a non-starter. 'I can't have pets in my apartment.'

'Then borrow one, befriend one,' suggested Maria patiently.

I left the consultation feeling the weight of the task. How does one create opportunities for physical contact without moving into dangerous territory? In addition I had been enjoying the spiritual dimension so much that it seemed to be a reasonable compensation for the absence of an intimate relationship. Wasn't the development of a heightened sense of spirit a major goal of living? Wasn't it the goal that would allow us serenity and peace and acceptance of our mortality? In the grand world of spiritual development, the physical dimension seemed tacky and small: great if you have it but ultimately not as worthy as the spiritual dimension.

Driving home I realised that however pleased I was with my spiritual dimension, I would still only be living a half-life if I did not engage with real people on earth. I also realised that I had been using a sort of spiritual snobbery as a defence mechanism to avoid living a full and exciting life. I felt a surge of energy. Suddenly re-establishing a normal relationship with Robert before he left Ireland became a matter of urgency. I pulled over to ring him on his mobile. Happily he was still in the country and planned to spend a few more days in Dublin before moving on. I was able to apologise for my behaviour, which he had not noticed, and take him around the city, up the mountains and cook big dinners for him. We went through my photo albums and talked about John with laughter and sadness. His open, enthusiastic company was a delight and I was able to send him off with deep gratitude for the change he had brought into my life.

*

Robert's visit had a powerful impact and left me feeling much stronger. My fears over the absence of a relationship eased off and the weeping and emotional overreactions faded. It was hard to work out how a short visit from my stepson and a brief conversation with Maria could have wrought such change but there was no mistaking the difference in myself. Shortly afterwards I decided to try salsa dancing in the city centre on the grounds that it would be a new and distracting interest. It also bore no relation to any other part of my life in Dublin now or in the past. The idea was a bit nerve wracking at first – me, a middle-aged woman without a partner, going to dance classes alone was excessively daunting and I was half-hoping I wouldn't find a suitable class.

'Don't be silly,' Warren advised during one of our periodic phone conversations. 'Get out there and try it.'

As it turned out the class was inclusive and entertaining. It was also the tip of the lively salsa network in Dublin that encompasses all ages and dancing abilities. I couldn't create a new relationship but I could at least break out of an isolating version of widowhood and dance.

35

ENDING THE GRIEF

In December 2005, approaching the fifth anniversary of John's death, I decided to end my grief by declaring it over. Although I experienced few identifiable symptoms of grief, I sensed it was still defining my life in a subtle way. I did not know what to expect from this declaration but at the very least I hoped it would provide me with a different perspective on life. For five years I had been a widow archetype; my thought patterns, behaviours and responses had come from within a paradigm of grief and bereavement. Initially my version of widowhood had been closed and restricting; as time went on, it had become more open and fluid but, as long as I could define myself as a widow, I would continue to have an excuse to avoid full interaction with the world whenever I was anxious or upset. It was time to withdraw that option altogether.

I had needed widowhood, particularly in the first two years after John's death when it had been critical to my survival. For the next three years, grief had motivated me to continue my convoluted journey of self-exploration and self-discovery. During that time I had dismantled many emotional patterns that had influenced my responses throughout my life and, when I used the techniques Brenda and Cath had taught me, I could erase internal obstacles and ease troubles. Therefore, I believed, I had exhausted the trials and challenges of widowhood. It was time to shift the focus of my life. I was healthy, calm and busy; I was writing full-time, dancing, travelling, socialising, hill-walking and gardening. Now it was time to capitalise on the knowledge and skills I had accumulated over the previous five years and start up some new adventures in living.

*

'It wouldn't suit everyone to declare their grief over,' said Maria when I saw her next, 'but it suits you. You are ready to let your intellect guide you now. For the last five years you have been like the Hanged Man in the Tarot, who is depicted as hanging upside down from a tree staring at stones; the story is that he remained there until he got it,' she explained.

The Tarot image of the Hanged Man is that of a person suspended from a tree by one foot; interpretations generally suggest that it relates to concepts of surrendering control, accepting knowledge, going with the flow of emotions, or taking action by not taking action.

For five years I certainly felt as if I had been hanging upside down from a tree, doing nothing until I 'got it'. On the face of it, I had not been completely dormant: I had moved country, travelled, published two books, changed careers and bought a house, amongst other things. Yet my memory of these five years was that it had been a period of motionlessness and isolation; I had frozen myself out of society since John died and gone on an internal adventure with my grief. Grief had pushed me to my limits and brought me to dark, exotic, strange and uncomfortable places. As with all the most successful adventures, I had received critical help and support when I needed it, and I had learnt an immeasurable amount about myself. Some of what I had learnt I had picked up quickly and some of it I had laboured over at an excruciatingly slow pace but, as I had been under no time pressure, the pace had been my business. Now, after five years, I had at last 'got it', or at least enough of it to attempt trying to live a fully integrated life once more.

'Once you come down from the tree, the way you see the world will be transformed,' continued Maria. 'Over the past years you have been staying still, looking after yourself and putting good structures in place, like a gardener setting up a trellis. It's hard and boring but now think of the things you can grow on the trellis.'

The transformation was unmistakable. At the most practical level I had picked up skills that virtually guaranteed periods of total peace of mind when I applied them. My meditation skills could relax me and sometimes transport me to places of heightened self-awareness; I could also be still long enough to hear the strong inner voice that I had begun to accept was at the very core of my being. I had reliable techniques for identifying which emotions or responses belonged to me and which belonged to someone else, and this allowed me to develop a healthy degree of detachment without compromising compassion. I could listen to my body in order to identify signs that suggested I was under emotional stress and might need help; and I had learnt the elusive skill of taking quality time out from managing, controlling and organising my world and routine. On these results alone, the time spent hanging out of a tree upside down for five years had delivered.

I had not entered this five-year adventure voluntarily and there had been times when I would have been happy enough if I had not woken up in the morning. Fortunately I had found enough motivation to push on. There was no question in my mind but that I had been a very damaged person during this period. Yet now I did not feel damaged at all and believed I could at last apply the nebulous concept of 'healing' to the work I had done. I was often wary about using that term in conversation because it had prompted strong reactions more than once from friends or acquaintances who thought it implied false promise for curing physical problems through non-scientific means. However, now focussed on ending this most difficult phase of my life, I was confident that what had happened in the last five years had been an extensive and comprehensive healing process. The healing did not directly affect any physical ailments – although I have no doubt but that the combination of counselling and therapies I had used for five years had prevented serious illness, particularly in my digestive system and lungs. Any physical healing, however, was a spin-off rather than an expectation or even a hope; the healing I had constantly required was at an emotional, internal level.

I never believed there was anything odd or unusual about what I had gone through, except perhaps for the amount of time I took to explore my grief and the range of resources available to me. When Mike died in 1984, the doctor and the priest had been the only professional resources available to help the bereaved that I had known about and nothing would have induced me to turn to either.

The professional help I received when John died emanated mostly from the availability of relatively new services and new approaches to self-development and spirituality in Ireland and Australia. The range was extensive, from western medicine, Chinese medicine and homeopathy, to kinesiology, reiki, Amatsu massage and a therapy known as Aura Soma, which uses colour. The overview provided periodically by Maria and the regular sessions with Brenda and Cath Carter held this eclectic mix together. The whole package had suited me perfectly.

*

Shortly after I made the decision to end my grief, I had a dream in which the image of John was clearer than in any dream I had ever had before. He was there, in colour, and, for the first time since he died, there was no damage to his face. I could trace each feature with my finger. He was smiling; I was in tears. He continued smiling; my tears turned to wailing and I curled up on the ground. He did not budge, did not react, did not say anything, but just smiled; then, like a child who realises that the tantrum isn't working, I stopped crying and stood up. He went on smiling and I smiled back. As I stood facing him I could feel myself as a separate entity, strong and confident. When I woke up, the image and the feeling lingered so distinctly that it might as well have been real.

*

On 7 December, the fifth anniversary of John's death, I went up the Three Rock Mountain on the outskirts of Dublin to declare my grief over. The day was wild, wet and windy and the mountain was empty of people as I made my way up the tracks through the trees. Near the top I made my declaration to the wind and the rain. It was strangely easy to do; in fact I felt relieved to be finished with it.

'After this,' I announced to the wind, 'any neurosis is just plain neurosis, not connected with John's death.'

I imagined John applauding and saying, 'Thank God for that, you took your time' and smiling.

Well, glowing – because I did not believe or try to sense that he was John as I had known him any more. The essence of John was now a pure spirit who was out there with the rest of the unseen universe. He was no longer a spirit-man to whom I turned for help when life became too much, or a spirit-man to be drawn in to hover at the edges of my life, or even a spirit-man to help me find a car park. I would still call him John and give him a gender for convenience, but it was no longer necessary for me to imagine him as a person who was just out of reach. My John was truly dead and that part of my life was over. Now when I thought of him, I just glowed too; there was no need for words.

EPILOGUE

Although I did not know it at the time, there was one outstanding step to be made after I declared my grief over, and it took me another eighteen months to acknowledge it. Declaring my grief over on the fifth anniversary of John's death had been, in retrospect, the right move because it forced me to consider the world with a forward-thinking outlook. Nevertheless life continued to feel like hard work at times but I was prepared to accept that as a normal part of living. On reflection I had, in fact, forgotten a time when life rolled along in a pleasant way so, despite my best intentions, this adventure was not over yet. The breakthrough came in mid-2007 when Maria said once more that it was time to socialise beyond my comfort zone. And once more, I could feel the tears welling up: here again was that insurmountable challenge that involved random socialising, meeting new people and maybe having another romantic relationship. When I argued that I had a reasonable social life, Maria pointed out that there was little or no natural flow to it because I was not pursuing any activities that were pure fun; nor had I established my own community of friends and acquaintances in Ireland. Of course I had my family and old friends but this was subtly different to having a general community of acquaintances with shared interests. I had already come to the conclusion that it takes five years to build up an extended body of friends and acquaintances in a new country. However the bit about socialising and an absence of pure fun upset me because I felt it was true – and it suggested that I wasn't out of the woods yet, damn it!

A close family member gave me some advice: 'Get out there and chat to people without any agenda. Some will talk back, others won't. Some might even be rude. You might even make an eejit of yourself. But who cares? If you don't risk it, you won't get the rewards.'

I felt the usual wave of panic and resistance rising at this suggestion so, to minimise the anguish, I resorted to a strategy: I resolved to accept invitations to ten events where I would know few if any people, and set a target at each event of chatting to at least two people I did not know. I allowed for one snub and one embarrassment per event – which seldom if ever happened – but it created the psychological safety net I needed to get me through the terrifying moments before going out. The plan worked so well that one social event led to another and I lost count before I reached ten.

I also took up scuba diving once more and spent several months late in 2007 doing very little except developing my skills in diving in temperate Irish waters. I began to enjoy it so much that I lost interest in self-exploration. I also took up playing bridge, a game I had loved as a teenager and this also became a happy obsession. Both of these activities required working with other people, which meant I now had to make contacts and establish networks based on shared interests. By the seventh anniversary of John's death on 7 December 2007, laughter and natural fun were becoming integrated parts of my life once more and I was waking up in the mornings feeling happy and peaceful for no particular reason. These feelings were similar to the fleeting sensations I had experienced in sessions with Brenda and Maria but now they were sustainable and might continue throughout the normal routine of the day. It was no longer a struggle to focus my mind on the activity of the moment and that indefinable darkness that had coloured my view of the day or the week ahead had dissolved. Life was flowing easily and the only tough challenges were those usually associated with choices I was making in relation to work. Maybe this was, at last, the state of being I had been striving towards; maybe this was feeling 'normal' again and maybe this was where my adventure had been taking me.

*

Back in December 2000, if I had known it would take me seven years to feel happy and enthusiastic about life once more, I wonder if I could have simply found a more feminine way of doing myself in and saved myself from the prolonged pain. However, now that I am here, I am prepared to say that it was a most extraordinary adventure: one with hideous depths, some inexplicable excitement and an outcome that goes beyond peace into the realms of a delight and joy in life that I had fantasised about when I began to work with Cath Carter in January 2003.

John's death had not destroyed my life but it had smashed it into a thousand pieces; it had been up to me to rebuild my life and find a new, pleasant way of being in the world. It was the wonder of who John had been that, before he died, he made sure I had the means and the skills to rebuild my life from that point. Over the seven years, the rebuilding process had, at times, felt as mechanical as putting one block on top of another, slapping in some mortar and waiting until it hardened before moving on. Sometimes I wondered if my approach was too clinical or detached but I had to relearn how to interact with so many aspects of life and the step-by-step approach kept me going while I exposed and healed my deepest emotions.

The spiritual dimension was the critical part of the adventure. After that first conversation with Maria, I was able to consider John's life as one that began in infinity and would continue to infinity. For a long time it had been much more difficult to generate peaceful thoughts when I considered my own life in those terms because the daily reality was such a struggle. Now it is easy to use even the simplest meditation to remember in a convincing and pleasing way that my life is part of a much longer spiritual life. In addition, that subtle inner voice at the heart of myself, which was once only accessible via dreams, is no longer barricaded in by emotional or cultural history. Happily, however, I am under no illusions that escape into the bliss of the spiritual world is any substitute for real living; I have only one conscious life in this lifetime and I intend to make the most of it, which of course requires being grounded firmly in an earthy reality.

*

When I started writing this book, I wanted it to be of practical help to people facing the same challenges. I was fortunate in having so many people around me who advised and supported me as I explored the dimensions of grief. Perhaps because I was immersed in travel writing in the year after John died, I had the idea of writing a grief manual to help other people through it. This book happened instead.

Nevertheless, in the tradition of the travel writer, I have identified a few practical lessons, which I picked up along the way. Some of these lessons I learnt in time to make use of for myself; others I recognised the value of only in retrospect. I have included them here in no particular order and they are based on my experience rather than on academic research.

The first lesson was immediate and involved getting through the night and, fortunately, it was one I managed very early on. Lying awake in bed at three o'clock in the morning, restless and unable to calm my mind, the darkness, silence and loneliness threatened to exaggerate how dreadful I felt. I learnt to stop fighting this nightly occurrence, made sure my bed and pillows were extremely comfortable, wrapped myself in a warm duvet and used a dual-control electric blanket to keep the chill out of the empty part of the bed.

The pressure of administration after John died was very distressing and I did not handle it as well as I might have done. The oddest of organisations demanded a certified copy of the death certificate and the will to close John's file or account. I would recommend now to anyone in a similar position to make multiple copies of the death certificate and will, create a form letter to accompany the documentation, and keep a stack of business envelopes and stamps close to hand. As soon as someone asks for a copy of either or both, attach them to a form letter and send them off without discussion or thought – even if it is the second or third time they have asked for the same documentation.

The physically debilitating impact of grief was a terrible surprise. I had expected it to be tough but did not expect the degree of impact it had in reality. Most of the advice I received shortly after John's death related to taking exercise and eating healthy food to maintain energy levels. It was a major effort at times to adhere to the principles of good eating but I am thankful for the advice because it unquestionably helped to stave off long-term damage to my digestive system and lungs.

A less obvious lesson concerned my relationship with close family and friends. They were vital in helping to ease my way but I had to ensure that I did not confuse them with professional therapists. Before John died, I had learnt how to ask for and accept help from people close to me. After he died, I gradually worked out that it would not be right or helpful to use my friends or family in the place of professional help over a prolonged period. With a little gentle nudging I accepted that I needed regular sessions with Brenda, my counsellor, and soon I learnt to 'park' the relentless troubles that were dominating my thoughts until I could release them in the safety of the hour I spent with her.

Another aspect of grief, which I did not deal with too well despite prior experience, was managing money and property in the early months. There were so many things to do that often I became careless about how I was spending money. I knew I was losing control but could not think of ways of managing it. I retrospect, I wish I had trained myself to use a few standard lines such as, 'I'll think about it for twenty-four hours', or 'I'll tidy/sort out/get rid of . . . in three months' time.' This might have given me time to think and be satisfied with my decision while remaining polite and in control.

A valuable lesson I picked up quickly came courtesy of the woman who said 'how can you laugh?' together with the subsequent advice from Warren. From this episode I learnt how to forgive people for saying odd things by accepting that they meant well but may have been unsure what to say.

At least they had said something because I found it quite difficult to be with people who said nothing at all.

It was more difficult to forgive myself for giving long, intimate answers about my bereavement to a semi-stranger; I never meant to do that but sometimes, unexpectedly, I would hear myself giving details of John's death to someone who probably had no desire to know about it. I could only assure myself that this was probably a standard manifestation of grief.

Mary and my counsellors helped me to work out that I needed to plan every anniversary or significant calendar day with utmost care, leaving little to chance for the first few years. The small ceremonies I created helped me to get through important – and potentially terrifying – days and mark them with events that left pleasant memories. On the second New Year's Eve after John's death when I ignored this advice, I got a terrible jolt and suffered as a result.

Another minefield for instant and unexpected distress was the supermarket and it took me so much by surprise that I did not develop a technique to help myself. Now, faced with the same situation again, I would wear dark glasses, play soothing music on an iPod, and carry lavender-scented tissues when I was going shopping for the first six months, particularly if it is Christmas; it was so hard walking past shelves of items containing products that were no longer required and buying food products in smaller sizes – and it was even harder when 'Merry Christmas Everyone' was playing in the background.

The final lesson I am including in this list is one that took me a few years to work out and I wish I had thought of it sooner. It relates to doing something occasionally that demands total absorption, even if it is a bit silly, like going on a roller coaster or on a fast boat trip or Space Mountain in Disneyland or, most thrilling and distracting of all, a tandem skydive; hurtling along at great speeds in relative safety provided brief but most welcome breaks from the relentless pressure of grief.

*

In spring 2008 I was in the company of a Vietnam veteran who suddenly began to have an episode similar to those John was having in the eighteen months before his death. The episode in the crowded city pub was provoked by an innocent reference to Vietnam the country and not the war. I did not know the man, who was in his late fifties, and certainly had no idea that he was a veteran but I recognised the symptoms immediately – the eyes filled with tears, the mouth slightly open unable to speak, the barely perceptible flinching in his body, the barely audible sobbing that comes from deep down, and the look, the terribly sad look that is a cross between horror and bewilderment. I sat with him as he drifted in and out of that strange semi-conscious state, which I associate with post-traumatic stress. He repeated himself, he repeated questions, he told half-stories, he grabbed his head when the voices of the Irish crowd turned into the voices of the Viet Cong, he stared at me without seeing me, then blinked, became flirtatious for a few minutes before disintegrating into a sobbing bundle once more. I stayed with him for a couple of hours, telling him he was safe and keeping my hand on his back using techniques I had learnt during reiki workshops. Never before had I seen anyone else going through an episode with exactly the same unbearable symptoms as John suffered. It makes me so sad that further generations of young men and women are returning from war bearing scars, which may not affect them with such obvious symptoms for several decades. My fervent wish for them is that they use every assistance to heal the wounds while they are still fresh and accessible.

As for myself, I feel cheerful, confident and in control, even in situations like that. I know my strengths and limitations and, if I become upset, I now know how to turn it into a positive experience. Of course I wish I knew then what I know now; perhaps I could have been much more comforting to John as he struggled through his final months but I know I could never have prevented his death. I do not know whether I can say for definite that I am finished with the grief or not but either way, it does not matter any more, I have no need to finish with it as such.

'Death is as much a part of living,' Maria had said the morning after John died. 'You will see the rightness of this in time.'

After eight years, the rightness of everything around John's death has fallen into place. There was no way of altering what had happened but my grief had led me on a journey that had become far more than a case of just making the best of a bad situation or learning to live with the loss. After meeting John in Papua New Guinea in 1986, we had many adventures together. The adventure that began with his death was yet another one and it has helped me to develop a powerful sense of myself. While I would not wish the detail of my own adventure on anyone, I would wish anyone the sense of self that gets a thrill out of being alive regardless of the circumstances, good or bad.

ACKNOWLEDGEMENTS

My deepest appreciation and thanks must go to my family and close friends who supported me in ways that made great demands on them at times. It is not an exaggeration to say that my current good health and cheerful outlook on life can be related directly to all of their help over the past eight years. An extended circle of old and new friends also helped me to keep going and to start enjoying life again. Sometimes I was in a position to acknowledge their help immediately; sometimes they helped me without being aware of how important their assistance was at the time. I have deliberately mentioned very few people by name to protect their privacy but I hope everyone who supported me knows how much I appreciate everything they did.

I also wish to acknowledge the professional people who guided me through the tough times. I was immensely fortunate in finding them and am very thankful that they were so forthcoming and skilful in how they worked with me.

Many strangers helped me with a kindly word or gesture, which made random moments easier to handle. I can only thank them in a most general way here and hope that I treat other strangers with the same kindliness and courtesy.

Driving this entire experience were the qualities instilled from an early age. My parents, Sean and Sheila de Courcy, encouraged me to travel and seek out challenges, persevere when it got tough, explore interesting avenues and take calculated risks. I learnt that reading and researching the experiences of other travellers could contribute significantly to safe and satisfying journeys. For many years, I applied these lessons to geographical travel. It was a revelation that the same lessons could be applied with great effect to the complex emotional adventure I found myself in after John died. Therefore I wish to acknowledge them specifically for these gifts and to add my story to the literature for someone else to use as part of their own exploration.

Finally, of course, I must acknowledge John and all of the strange ways he helped me to achieve a remarkable outcome of this most extreme adventure.

BIBLIOGRAPHY

The Book of Runes, commentary by Ralph Blum. Angus and Robertson, 1984.

Simple Buddhism, by C. Alexander Simpkins and Annellen Simpkins, Tuttle Publishing, 2000.

Best We Forget, by Bernard Clancy. Indra publishing, 1998.

BIBLIOGRAPHY